THE THEATRE

THE THEATRE

by

Stark Young

❧ ❧

LIMELIGHT EDITIONS   NEW YORK

First Limelight Edition, January 1986

For permission to reprint certain passages in this book thanks are due to the editors of the *Yale Review, The New Republic, Theatre Arts Monthly Magazine, The Bookman*.

Library of Congress Cataloging-in-Publication Data
Young, Stark, 1881–1963.
  The theatre.

  Reprint. Originally published: New York: Hill and Wang, 1958. (A Dramabook)
  1. Theatre. 2. Drama. I. Title. II. Series:
Dramabook.
PN1655.Y6   1985   792   85–18206
ISBN 0-87910-046-X (pbk.)

To Eric Bentley

CONTENTS

THE THEATRE

THE THEATRE ART

THE GOLDEN DAY in the theatre would dawn when the dramatist himself directed his play, with actors capable of expressing entirely the meaning that he intends, and a designer whose settings and costumes bring the whole event to its final perfection.

This blest occasion would exhibit the creator in the art of the theatre working straight, using one medium directly, as any other artist does, as the painter does, the architect, the musician. But such a day never dawns; and the process by which a piece of theatre art comes into existence is nothing so single or direct. We have first the idea or the matter that is to be expressed in this particular medium that we call the art of the theatre. This medium in turn consists of a number of other mediums that compose it, such as the play, the acting, the décor. And these mediums involve other artists, the actor, the director, the designer, the musician, and depend on them. The art of the theatre is the most complex of all arts.

The dramatist is the most important figure in the eternal theatre, the theatre that outlasts one generation only, that goes on from epoch to epoch. Actors may build up styles, leave behind them traditions and theories of acting; designers of settings and costumes may illuminate their province, leave drawings after them, and even, as in the case of the Bibiena family, stamp for generations the mark of their style on the theatrical scene. But acting is transitory, a lively record while it lasts, lustrous, fading, blotted out by a few stretches of the trampling years; and the designer's art lives only, or for the most part, by its shadow or idea. Only the play can, as it stands, endure, according to its merit or fortune, and two centuries afterward be seen in its own body. The dramatist, too, nearly always supplies the essential idea behind a theatre work. He gives the theme; and creates the theme in terms of life. Of all the parts of a work in the art of the theatre, his affords the closest and most securely grounded application to life. It is therefore only natural that ninety-nine out of a hundred books on the theatre have been really about the drama; and that most of the study of the subject, outside of the profession, has been concerned with plays.

But in the immediate occasion—an evening at a theatre—the dramatist's share takes its place with the other elements that go to make up the art. Along with the acting, the décor and the directing, goes the drama itself—all make up what is not dramatic literature, not acting, not designing or directing but one art: the theatre art. The question as to which of these elements or parts that contribute to this theatre art contributes most, is for the moment unimportant; we may say that each goes to make a living whole, exactly as we may say that the parts of a man's body are all seen alive together, all make up the body, which consists of and lives by them all.

Life, the energy, the living essence—Pirandello's "stream of life," Bergson's "vital urge"—goes on, finding itself bodies or forms to contain and express it. Behind whatever is dramatic lies the movement of the soul outward toward forms of action, the movement from perception toward patterns of desire, and the passionate struggle to and from the deed or the event in which it can manifest its nature. Behind any work of art is this living idea, this soul that moves toward its right body, this content that must achieve the form that will be inseparable from it. A perfect example in any art arrives not through standards but when the essential or informing idea has been completely expressed in terms of this art, and comes into existence entirely through the medium of it. This is perfection, though we may speak of a perfection large or small. When a form is found that will completely express an idea that is largely applicable to human experience and therefore largely significant, we have a large perfection; and a high perfection when the work of art is what Longinus would call an echo of elevation of mind—μεγαλοφροσύνη—and in its presence the mind "in the height of its rapture exults and feels a sort of command, as if it itself produced what it has only been perceiving."

Play, acting, design, directing, music make up the theatre art. But so little is that recognized or remembered that, though we speak of the play or the acting or some such element in what we have been to see, we have no name for the whole instance. Our sense of the theatrical event as a whole must suffer for this lack of a word. In this discussion, in order to avoid such a poor phrase as an "instance of creation in the art of the theater" we shall say "a theatre work" as we say a painting, a symphony, a drama, a poem.

With us in America just now the theatre is at a certain sag. Where five years ago* there was excitement over new impulses and explorations into fresh forms, there is in this present lull only what is at best a kind of marking time. Then there was a great asking, How? how? how? how shall this be?—but now there is little. So that now, while we have leisure to let our eyes wander over it, may be a good time for a little book of notes on the theatre art as a whole. We may consider the various arts or elements that make it up and the sensuous avenues that lead to it.

But first there is the matter of seeing the theatre as an art at all.

* Around 1927.

2

AN IMPURE ART

To SEE ANYTHING as art means that you do not see it as a duplicate of something in life. It means that you see it as complete in itself. You judge its truth by its intentions, its essential idea. It means that you allow it to be free of its material, and perceive that it uses the material—as Corot does a landscape, El Greco a human body, Beethoven a state of mind or mood—to express an idea, a soul; that it does what it chooses to do, forcing the material to its own purpose, which is to find a form for a content.

What makes the theatre so difficult to see as an art is the impurity of its medium.

For purity, music, and architecture come first among the arts. They profit most from the advantage that is enjoyed by an art in which resemblance plays no part and the medium can express pure idea or quality. They are obviously the most ideal of the arts. The musician through tone, tempo, pitch, and rhythm establishes designs or bodies or patterns that are the essence and the soul of the experience that he wishes to create. The architect employs line and mass to create a form that is free of every likeness and is judged by nothing outside of architecture. Painting is in general less free. Certain modern painting has essayed pure color forms free of all likeness and expressive in themselves. But painting fundamentally touches on likeness; it derives from our definite visual experience, and follows the world around us, in which we see forms not as abstractions but as stubborn facts embodied in reality. Where a musician can give us despair and loneliness itself, a general and essential experience, a painter can give us the experience only by means of a definite phenomenon, an instance out of life through whose representation a lonely despair may be aroused in us. The poet is free only after a fashion; he takes his subjects from life, so much of which consists of external facts, and to these facts he must to some extent at least be faithful. He is, furthermore, less free than the musician or the architect owing to the fact that his medium—words—is bound faster to actual associations, to connotations, than theirs, though they too, of course, must contend with something of the same thing in familiar and remembered forms and motives. But any one of these arts is pure compared to the theatre.

What pigment is to a painting and sound to music, the acting or the décor is to the art of the theatre. But the designer is an artist working through his own medium of the décor. His service to the theatre depends on his being himself an artist in his own art. And the actor complicates matters by being an artist himself, using a distinct and additional medium —his personality, body, and voice—to create his idea. He gives himself to the whole creation but he remains himself as well, or he would not be an artist and therefore not a fit medium for the whole idea. There is a further complication. The actor and the

acting constitute the medium by which the characters and their actions are converted into the art of the
theatre. The actor is a medium, as oil pigment is
Corot's medium; the material is the personage that is
portrayed, as the valley of water and trees and light
is Corot's material. The acting is a medium, the human action and character portrayed is the material.
But the actor conveying a man to us is himself a man.
John Barrymore acting Hamlet is a man as Hamlet
is. What the character does is a piece of human behavior, and what the actor does is behavior. Art and
nature, which is which? Where does one leave off and
the other begin? Which is the material, which the
medium? To make the distinction is not easy. Only
in the theatre does so much intervene between the
artist's idea and his expression of it.

To know that every work of art is complete in itself and free of its material is the beginning of any
understanding of art. About music and architecture
every one feels this freedom by mere instinct and by
experience with what these arts have offered him.
Nobody thinks Beethoven's *Ninth Symphony* good
because some of it sounds like a cuckoo, nobody
would object to Bach's "Coffee Cantata" because you
hear no grinding, roasting, and boiling. Only a
simpleton would praise a building because it looked
like a tree or a hat; and only an idiot say that
he wanted Bernini's façade of St. Peter's built to look
more like nature. Even in painting there are thou-
sands who allow Botticelli to distort the anatomy of
his Venus, raising the hips and lifting the body on to
the balls of the feet, tilting the head to one side, in
order to secure the idea that he wishes to create in

terms of design—a certain vision and an intellectual poetry that we know as his—and for the same end we will allow him to flatten, to blanch into pallor, his leaves and trunks and to outline with gold these unrealities in the form of trees.

Of trees, indeed, the painter may take what elements he chooses. He may render them faithfully, in a sort of noonday prose like Rousseau; or as a flat pattern in a mural composition like Giotto; he may turn them as Gainsborough does into textures like those of tapestry; he may follow Corot and make of trees only a home for dew and morning; or like some old Chinese painter he may set down the trees in a line whose quality expresses serenity or solitude or whatever idea the painter wishes. In every case you judge the painting by the tree only in so far as the painter's intention was resemblance or duplication of the tree. Only to judge the degree of success in the likeness, where likeness was intended, may you look from the work of art to the model or material.

We can at least try to avoid theories and conceptions that will cut us off from what a theatre work has to say and that set up obstacles to our response and enjoyment. If you say that Duse was bad in *Così Sia* because as the peasant woman she did not look like a peasant, you do one of two things—you either, because of some objection on artistic principle, hold yourself back from what you like, which is a limitation in your theory; or you find an argument for not liking what you fail to see or understand, which is only plausible obtuseness.

The wise thing to do at such a moment is to remind yourself that all arts rest on essentially the same basis, whatever makes sense about one art makes sense about another, so far as fundamentals go. In your Duse impasse, then, ask yourself if your objection, namely that the artist did not contrive a likeness, would hold in other arts. In painting, for instance, is Veronese's "Marriage at Cana" bad because these Jews of the first century are dressed as Venetians of the sixteenth? Or is the sculpture of the Egyptians inferior because it is not anatomical? The answer is that in each case, the painter, actor, and sculptor, according to his genius and his special art, made what use he chose, and at his own peril, of his material.

The history of any art is a history of man's states of mind and spirit, not of the objective world around him. To be ignorant of that is to be ignorant of the theatre as an art, and leads to a mere muddle of resemblances and recognitions, a confusion between life and the theatre, contradictions about naturalness and artifice, and—what is profoundly important—blindness to such ideas as may require a new method or form to express them.

3

AVENUES

THE THEATRE ART has several voices no one of which is necessarily more important than the rest. One is the word, the spoken symbol of an idea. One lies in the realm of music, the avenue of the ear, and uses tone, rhythm, tempo to express what is to be conveyed to the audience. The third is the visual, what we see there on the stage, what speaks to our eyes and through them conveys to us an idea.

The importance or expressiveness of each of these languages, the word, the music, the visual, will vary according to what is to be expressed, since one quality or idea is best expressed in words, another in gesture or color, another in sound; not every kind of pleasure—as Aristotle said of tragedy—can be required of any one of these, but only its own proper pleasure. The importance of each of these will vary, too, according to the man who receives it; for one man the word above all else is what can rouse the life by which a work of art is alive for him; for another the ear is the liveliest approach; for a third the eye brings most excitement and response. That is as it may be—every man in his own humor and born talents. But one thing we must keep clear. Nobody must make the common and natural mistake of thinking that in the theatre it is the word above all else that talks.

As for the average man and his senses, he can be shown how little he hears, if you take the unfruitful pains of showing him up. You could soon prove to him that at the most only a tenth of what a musician hears in a symphony of Beethoven's will register in his ear. The tiny beetle for delicate sounds heard from afar makes him a sorry figure; and the image of an Indian hearing a distant message by leaning down above a flowing stream, proves to him what he has lost in the keenness of this sense. As for his eyes you can demonstrate that he does not know that shadows are bluer at one hour than another and that what he calls gray is a strong violet. He confuses rose with red; he will not have seen it when an architect has lengthened his panel to make the elevation of his choir wall soar above the reredos. When we come to words demonstration is harder. Words are in a more private and inner region and are only symbols of the images and actions of our brains. Words are a sort of secret science for him, like the plumber and his operations in the dark or the doctor's veiled knowledges. And so, since it is harder to confront him with what he gets from words, your man may conclude that words mean what they mean; in the kingdom of words, he thinks, men are all born equal. But even there he has no ground to stand on. Even if his wits and his culture could retain all word meanings in their exact propriety, provided they had any, he would find that meanings themselves will not stay in place, not even the names of the plainest objects. Grass, which means a certain form of vegetation no doubt, means also to one a happy verdure and to another the frailty of life; and there are those to whom coal, plain useful carbon in the furnace room, means mere blackness or heat and those to whom it spells the cost of living. And there are numberless words, words like *beauty*, *endeavor*, *ardent*, *inclination*, that have numberless degrees of meaning to as many users; to these many minds they are, as Euripides' Tiresias said of the meaning of Bacchus, not violations but fulfillments, and are expressive of each follower according to his nature.

But whether an average spectator responds most readily to words, sound or sight or whether one art is more expressive than another, is not the point, which is that each one of these is an avenue and each art a language in itself, and that every art is justified in its existence by the extent to which it alone can express what no other art can. On the same basis we can say that in the theatre a gesture added to a word is justified finally in so far as it expresses something that the word cannot express; or that in a cry of joy the tone or pitch says one thing, a word in the midst of it clinches or defines the nature of the joyous emotion, and both together bring us more fully into play. The quality of an action may be intensified, or varied at least, by putting it in the midst of a different setting. The figures of men fighting before a gray wall, or against red curtains or in a black empty space, what a different thing is said in each case!

The function of words, we all know. They express nothing except by agreement. No words except the onomatopoetic, only the *thuds*, *buzzes*, *booms*, and so on of the dictionary, which merely reproduce the thing they talk about, are anything but symbols that, by usage or consent, stand for ideas and things. But the word specifies, focuses, directs. In the midst of tears the word *grief*, or *homesickness*, gives a more definite point to the underlying thing the tears express, in the same way that a title on a musical composition—*Reverie*, for example, *In the Elysian Fields*, *The Garden in the Rain*—directs the whole experience that the music expresses to a special application, and so gives us a starting point that is more concrete and that may gratify a certain side of us.

Words, too, by the memories they arouse, the things they connote, achieve infinite, inexpressible meanings for us. And words in combination, by this living surprise of their use at an artist's hands, enjoy the resources not only of what they reflect upon each other when set together thus, but also of the accompanying rhythm and tone, with all the vitality that this implies. The purpose of every work of art is to arouse in us the experience that the artist had and strives to re-create; the purpose in every use of a word is to arouse the life in it, to recapture its freshness and that first glory that it had when a living need created it. And lastly, there remains the power of certain words as mere sounds, without onomatopoetic qualities and without necessary associations with what they represent, though often that, too, swiftly follows after: *desiderium, sidera,* θάλασσα, *prière, flores,* or, *rain,* or *colonnade,* the very sound itself of these moves into the sense and takes us.

But the word itself, made up of letters as it is, cannot in the theatre of all places be divorced from its sound. The harmony of speech, recitation, voice, brings the word-medium of the theatre into the realms of music. There is too, and quite divorced from vocal tone, the time interval in speech: the distance at which our ear receives a word from one person that answers some word of another's a moment before, is as much a part of the idea as the word itself. The tempo and the tone are languages quite as the word is, sometimes one of the three is more important to the idea, sometimes another. The plain word *no* means simply negation or refusal, but by tempo and vocal tone other meanings are added. When a character asks, Are you certain of his guilt? and another answers *no*, he is speaking two languages, one the language of the word, which in this case remains the same; the other of music, by which the meaning can be changed at will. If he says *no* at once in a clear tone, *no* fifty seconds after the question and in a shrill tone, *no* one minute after the question in an angry tone, and so on, he is plainly saying different things, things of which the word is only a small part. The gradations and values of sound in the theatre are in their way as infinite and inexhaustible as music is.

In a cultivated theatre the region of the ear, of music, is by contrast with that of the eye, of the visual, a livelier means of expression. Not for nothing does the word *aesthetic* go back, through the idea of perception, to the Greek word *to hear*. It involves all the qualities of speech, tone, tempo, rhythm, accent, and emphasis, and also the use of music itself wherever the theatre artist finds that his idea can at a certain point be best expressed through music. Where the painter can give us only a panorama like a body of soldiers marching, and the poet only words about it, set, if you like, in a

certain expressive rhythm, the musician can put marching into us, can lift up the soles of our feet. But this is
obvious and a commonplace about the art. Music, too,
of all arts draws most deeply on the stored up experience in us that belongs to the race, an ageless biological
memory, only at the surface pricked and ticketed by
our individual life. Things for which there are no
words, which rule us without sharing their counsels
with us, which have no outlines or patterns in our
thinking but which move in us like the wind through
the world, which are ourselves indeed and carry us
beyond ourselves, all these sound can express or arouse.
Music is the art most ready to live within us. Music
alone of all the arts can express at the same time both
the life of our senses and the life of our desires.

Of the visual side of the theatre the element that is
nearest to sound or music lies in the acting, and in
that side of the acting that we might indeed call its
visual music. By this I mean the flow of movement and
gesture, of stage position, of the ensemble and the
single figure, of the continuity of rhythm that the
actor's body establishes. This I mean at the moment to
be considered as separate from action or gesture that
imitates the actions we might see the characters do in
life, though that too has its visual music. I mean movement as in itself expressive, expressive as the movement
in an architectural façade is, or as the sea's lines are
expressive. Familiar gestures on the stage may be expressive through the meanings that we have learned to
attach to them in life. But a gesture may in itself move
and persuade us, quite apart from any resemblance
and quite without its being what is called natural at
all. It may have about its line, its rhythm, its cadence

and completed design, something that draws us along with it and persuades us to its idea as a passage in music does.

Acting in general of every kind—in addition to this visual music of movement—establishes what is after all the most convincing element in the theatre. It speaks to our eyes by showing them the people and the actions that we see in life. Words may convey the characters' thoughts and may be in themselves a kind of action; music may arouse the liveliest and most deeply essential response; settings and atmosphere may stir, heighten or transport us. But the persons that we see, what we see them do, and the events they share in, these are what give the theatre its hold and its reality; these are the starting point for our response, however far great words, music, and scene may illuminate and go beyond them. Even in an extreme instance of the drama of inaction, Chekhov's *The Cherry Orchard*, for example, what counts is the picture of the characters and the action they do not do; and to this picture the words spoken are only a murmur of life beneath the living image.

The importance of the décor, of the settings and costumes that are involved, will, naturally, vary in importance with the occasion. One play depends heavily on the dramatic rightness of the setting, on a certain dramatic harmony or contrast in its scene, another will be independent of the setting; one theatrical idea will be expressed more by setting and atmosphere than by words or acting, another can no more be expressed by the visual scene than a tariff law could be said in music or a proverb in architecture. By way of décor, however, is brought to the theatre no small portion of the resources of painting, sculpture, and architecture, and the power of each to express what it alone of all arts can. And through the settings and costumes the theatre affords the gamut of textures, involves our sense of touch, and all the experience connected with that sense.

There are forms of theatrical art, celebrations, ballets or revues that lean heavily on spectacle; and there is a play now and then that depends for its point on settings and costumes that express an epoch or a locality dramatized into the play. But in general the décor is far behind both the play and the acting as an expressive medium in the theatre, as is proved by the fact that, though good acting often saves a bad play from failure and a good play is sometimes actor-proof, settings and costumes alone have rarely carried poor acting and poor drama to success.

All these sensuous resources, then, are avenues by which the theatre draws us out and enters into us. All these various arts, each a medium in itself, contribute to the theatre medium's inclusiveness and range.

◆§ 4 §◆

TRANSLATIONS

WHY IS IT that when a producer like the late Beer-
bohm Tree is at endless pains and expense to give us
a section of Henry VIII's palace as it looked, exactly
reproduced, and puts within it figures with costumes
of the utmost accuracy, we feel so little call to admire?
It is all an excellent duplication, it is all what the real
Henry lived amidst. But it hardly strikes us as art at all.

This is because architecture that is a copy in paint
and canvas of an original in stone, remains after all a
copy, a photograph of architecture. It can be admired
as such. But it is only that, and remains only that until
it is expressed in terms of this new art, the theatre, of
which it has become an element.

Architecture, painting, costume, music, literature,
all these arts enter into that of the theatre; architecture
and painting and costume as a part of the décor, literature as the spoken drama; music either as expressive in
itself, giving us the dramatic experience where nothing
else might serve so well, or as a means of release, of
breaking down the entity, the bounds of control,
within which we try to hold ourselves, and drawing us
into the infectious life of the moment.

But none of these arts can exist alone to itself in the

28

theatre. Either it becomes theatrical or it remains extraneous, the mere injection of another substance into the body of this art, without making it a living part of that body, as flesh introduced into our stomachs is made into our flesh before it is a part of us. An architectural façade before it becomes theatre has to be restated in theatrical terms, which include the play's dramatic mood, the space element in the theatre—that special *optique du théâtre* of which we read—the presence of the actors, the stage lighting, the time elements, and so on. A costume taken from a Holbein portrait of King Henry must be restated in theatre terms before it becomes a part of this theatre art, precisely as Holbein had to restate the original clothes in painting terms.

Exactly the same thing is true of literature. A word, a sentence, spoken in the theatre has from that moment been re-created in new terms and must stand a new test. It is no longer a word on a page but is translated now into another medium, the theatre, where it may pass from poor literature to at least better theatre or shrink from good literature to very poor theatre. At all events it is theatre now; the sound of the actor's voice is added to it and the time values that he creates, the audience is added, the stage spaces and the positions of the persons on it with regard to each other, the lights, the scene itself. It is obvious that the word *exquisite* differs when spoken before a thousand people from what it is in a book; and that if four people standing in a line say *The honor of the family is lost*, the thing said is not what the sentence repeated on a printed page would say. All writing must be created anew and something thereby added that was not there before, a new body with a new soul, before it passes from literature into the theatre art.

What is true of these arts passing into theatre is in the same way true of the material out of life that must suffer this translation into new terms. Material does not become art until it is restated thus; which is what Congreve meant when he said that if a poet should steal a dialogue of any length from the extempore discourse of the two wittiest men upon earth, he would find the scene but coldly received by the town.

Art, indeed, can be thought of as a restatement of an experience in one part of life in terms of another part of life.

Byron, riding for hours in the pine wood that joins Ravenna to the Adriatic shore, might take into himself the quiet there, the immemorial spaces of the sea beyond the tree trunks, the light so still and serene under the trees, and put it into his poem, not the descriptive record of it only, the poetic picture, but the essential quality, which would be evinced in the peculiar music of his verses, their tone and mood. Gluck might take what the moon at night in its clear sky aroused in him and restate it in music, another section of life. In conduct, the moral life, it could be the same. A man contemplating a vile, base action might, after having life given to him by a noble music or some grave beauty in a building of Sansovino's, find himself unwilling to do the act; what he lived in Sansovino he wishes to live in himself and his actions.

On the other hand a man after reading Byron's poem might experience in the pine wood at Ravenna a fuller response, discovering in his moment there a deeper quality of perfection in living. This reverses the matter and completes the point. Life, rising in us, discovers forms for its soul, in acts, in ideas, in art. The life expressed in one of these parts of life can find also forms for itself in other parts.

A work of art is either alive or dead. It is alive when the life in it to be expressed has found a body in the art involved, a body composed of its elements. Otherwise, whatever the idea, the result as a work of art does not exist. A picture of a young visionary lying dead from the poison his despair has brought him to, may be pathetic only because of the story we get from it, and may give us a species of literary excitement but only that. The essential idea has not found its expression in painting terms, in qualities of color, line, brush, and so on. Blood smeared on the door of a church might arouse us to a terrific response, but none of us would say that it had any architectural existence. The shock of it was anatomical, not architectural. In the theatre the same.

In the reverse direction, if we see a work of art and do not feel the life in it passing into us, restated in terms of our natures or ideas or acts, we can hardly be said to have seen it at all; we have not responded to it. We have missed its content, which is there to be received; for the life in it is not strange to the life in us. St. Paul's saying that we live in one flesh—ἕν τῷ σῶμᾳ—is not alone true of human beings but of men and the arts as well, they are parts of one another's bodies.

A man's body is alive throughout only in so far as

it translates into its own kind whatever is taken into it; what is not thus translated is not a part of it. So in the theatre what is alive is organic, it partakes throughout of the same tissue, the same nature; every part of it has its due tendency toward the whole.

◆§ 5 §◆

THE DRAMA

THE PLAY is the most important element in the theatre. Sometimes the acting or the décor will count for more than the play, but it is the play in most cases that gives the idea on which the whole is built and that creates the dominant quality of the whole effect. It is the play that contributes the guiding mind, the essential idea which the *régisseur*, however great an artist he may be, tries to express through the theatrical medium that he works in. From the play the actors draw their chief notion of the characters they create. From the play as a rule the designer takes his start, however short he may come of it or how far go beyond. And it is the play that endures where scenery fades and rots, the pattern of the color and the miracle of the lighting long since forgotten.

This is especially true in the English-speaking theatre. We have no solid body of tradition and nothing of what you might call a theatre world, not in the serious theatre at least; nor have we any system of revivals of the same play throughout a season or from season to season. In the theatre of revues and musical comedies it is different, what is done in a certain kind of scene will be repeated in another scene of the same kind; there is a language of gesture, dance, and gag that keeps going and alive quite as much as the words of the pieces do and sometimes more than the words. But in our serious theatre what survives is words. A play remains as a text, and the gestures and movement that were once a part of it are lost, and in a very few seasons after, a production of it would have to be entirely re-created.

Other theatres are different, no doubt, certainly the French is. That theatre has for centuries been centered in Paris. From the time of *le Roi Soleil*, the Parisian theatre has had volumes of unwritten matter that is as much a part of the plays produced in the theatre as the words are. There are positions, tricks, tones, pieces of stage business for Molière's plays that survive from Molière's own performances. And, to take more modern examples, the Guitry plays are so much a part of Paris and Paris of them that many of their scenes could not be produced at all from the text; only from seeing what is done in them on the French stage could we present them with anything like satisfaction. But even at that, in France as with us, it is the text that is most likely to be handed on.

A play consists, obviously, of plot, characters, dialogue. Of these the theatre of modern times has centered on character as the revealing element, as that part of drama by which most is expressed. Most people at present would go so far as to say that character is the all important and first consideration in a drama; it is almost a commonplace to say so. Such a theory would be expected. It falls in with our general drift toward detail instead of finality of outline, and with our general spinelessness and weak touch. It is like the color, the shading, the mood in so much modern painting, all very well in their way, but something more of pattern and robust composition added to it would be a better sign of strength. Great character creation is a fine thing, obviously; but it is just as obvious that much fiddling and fooling and faking comes easy to character writing, and that such writing is always in danger of running into mere psychological patter and subdivision on subdivision without reality of any kind. The fictionistic trash of much modern character study a blind man ought to see.

"Character," Mr. Galsworthy goes so far as to say, "is situation," which I think is true, if you mean that a character fully created carries with it the action expressive of him at a given moment. But when he says that character is plot, he must be wrong. A set of characters fully explored and created in quality and motive and situation, if you like, and all taken together, do not imply the plot. The combination of events that will arise involves not only these characters and their actions but their relation to the life around them and to the complete dramatic idea that the dramatist wishes to express, and uses these characters and actions and events to express.

In the greatest plays the permanent value rests, on the whole, on both plot and characterization; in plays below the highest grade it rests sometimes on one, sometimes on the other, though in modern plays of this rank it is characterization on which the permanent value is based. It is true also that in many a modern play what interests us almost entirely is the characters, just as in modern buildings what may interest us is some quality or special element presented. But this does not mean that such a play might not hold its place

longer or such a building not be more important archi-
tecturally if these characters roundly achieved a plot
to sum up themselves and their actions, and if these
special partial elements achieved a significant outline
and architectural mass.

Great character creation is a fine thing in a drama,
but the sum of all its characters is the story that they
enact. Aristotle puts the plot at the head of the dramatic elements; of all these he thinks plot the most
difficult and the most expressive. And he is right. Not
that every plot stands first, or any and every plot is
more important than the characters in the play; any
plot counts only in so far as it is expressive. But the fact
remains, nevertheless, that the plot is the most important of all the elements in drama because of them all it
can be most completely expressive of the characteristic
idea behind the play. And by this process:

The artist has an idea, an essential quality, a content, to express in terms of a play. Ready at hand he
has, as means of expression, the life or atmosphere or
manners portrayed, the sentiments, thoughts, and emotional reactions characteristic of human beings; he can
work in terms of these and of his characters, their
actions and the plot or story. He puts his idea into each
of these terms, as the human characteristic is expressed
in the various parts of a man's body. Of these terms
the most important—because they express most to us
—are character, action, and plot. A man's character is
most apparent in what he does or does not do; our
character appears in our actions. The dramatist discovers creative actions, actions expressive of his characters. A plot in a play derives from these actions
brought into combination, as they meet and cross one

another, in the world of life that they embody and express. If the characters express themselves in their actions, and the sum of their actions implies the plot, it follows that the plot includes, or can at least include, them both, and can be therefore of all the elements in the play the most inclusive, and therefore most largely and completely expressive of the play's essential idea or quality.

People go on telling us, nevertheless, that the plot is secondary, and they prove it, if by no other argument, by citing the supposedly well-known fact that there are only a few plots, after all, for dramatists to use. Thirty-six plots there are in all, according to the scholars, we are told. This business about few plots, or thirty-six plots, goes back more than a century and a half to Gozzi's famous category. But Gozzi said nothing of plots, he said thirty-six situations. Schiller, so Goethe tells us, thought Gozzi had allowed too small a number, but when he came to count, he could not find so many. Georges Polti in his book, *Les 36 Situations Dramatiques*, developed Gozzi's idea. But the point here is that, while the number of situations may be so limited, the plots to be woven around them are innumerable. And a plot, moreover, does not mean a mere loose story, but a story in its exact dramatic gradations.

So common is the prejudice in favor of character as the leading element in drama that you can hear the characters spoken of as creation, the plot as invention. A foolish distinction; compared to the characters in a play the plot is only creation in larger terms, since the author starts with qualities which he creates into characters, whom, in turn, he creates into actions and these actions into a plot; so that the plot is only an extension of his creation. In a poor example plot may appear as mere invention because of its lack of connection with the characters, in which case it seems only a vehicle for them, or merely to be tagged on to keep things going. Or it may appear as mere invention because of its final expressiveness; the artist might seem merely to have come upon it, as men come upon the force of steam or the use of electricity. But the more inclusive and expressive the plot the more the degree of creation. In a good play the plot is the most inseparable element in it; in such a case there is no locale, character or action that would mean the same if isolated to itself and seen without the plot. The plot is the most elusive element in a play to regard in itself because it is the hardest to isolate, to see separately; and at the same time it is the most distinct and the most final in its effect. The plot is the ultimate element by which we can discern the essential character of each individual play as distinguished from all other plays. This point, despite the critical theories about character and plot, will be proved at once by any history of dramatic literature: in any account of a series of plays the historian will finally distinguish one from another by a statement of their plots.

Is then the plot of *Othello* its most important element? Yes. The characters exist, they act; they have a certain relationship among themselves as embodiments of human nature and of the dramatist's ideas; the sum of their relationships and actions determines the plot. Is the plot of *Le Misanthrope* the most important element in it? No. But that only amounts to saying that Molière was not able to create a plot that would completely embody his idea, which he was obliged to express largely through his characters, who exist in their quality rather than in what they do. Chekhov's *The Three Sisters* on the other hand is theatre, as experiment has proved, but the idea is most expressed in character and atmosphere, and in what its people do not do; this last constitutes a kind of negative plot that is the strongest element in our impression of the play.

What impresses me most about the work of Eugene O'Neill is his power at his best to create a plot outline that in itself has shape, idea. In this respect *The Hairy Ape*, of all his plays, comes first. In that play the story itself is a simple line that in itself expresses the entire idea. Hank, the Stoker, exploded from that job into the world, tries to join the I.W.W., he is kicked out of that, he goes into the great ape's cage and is crushed to death—neither man nor beast has a place for him. So completely expressive is the pattern of this plot that neither the characters nor the dialogue seem essential to the idea. It may be said, too, that Eugene O'Neill's great gift is most evident in the bold figure of his plots. His men and women are often mere symbols or type puppets to carry out the action, and what they say is often type speech in dialogue that is obviously to serve the purposes of the story or dramatic theme. The strong stir of life that this dramatist can often arouse derives from the fact that he gives us the sense of action and of an intense current of emotion rather than of close and detailed observation or individual character likeness. A part of his reputation is due to the ease with which people can convey the idea of one of his plays by recounting the mere bare plot.

Fables, whose life is long when they are good, are

all plot. In a fable like that of *The Prodigal Son* the characters are wholly action, we know nothing of them but what taken all together they did, we know nothing but the plot, and this expresses the whole idea. The history of great fables as the undying vehicles of ideas proves their consummate worth. And finally, to leave art and come to actual men and women, we can say that in the case of a man like St. Francis of Assisi it is largely his genius for doing things wonderfully expressive of himself and his idea, that makes him to this day so real to us; and, furthermore, we may say that there is no character in history who is not most remembered by his story.

Of the four moods in drama, tragedy, comedy, farce, and melodrama, the tragic must always be greater than any other because it most of all brings to bear upon the atom of our human life the infinite universe; and because it includes more of our life, which, whatever happy emphasis it may have had in its long course, is grounded in the tragic, it begins in another's pain and ends in death. All things pushed to their bounds are tragic, for despite the wills and passionate desires that we exert upon them, they have an end at last, and at last are taken from us. The tragic in drama has had many definitions, the struggle of the individual will against eternal law, the struggle of the good with the good, and so on, as we may see in any primer of the subject. In older styles the image of tragedy is always death, the death of the hero is the conclusion of the struggle. It was upon the shock of death that the famous metaphysical comfort of the philosophers ensued, the state in which we rise above ordinary considerations of personal advantage and contemplate the whole, with our passions quieted, our tempers purged, our spirits lifted with the sense of wisdom gained. In later forms the tragic can be death, as in *Ghosts*, or the closed passage in *The Three Sisters*, mere negation and defeat of life. Or it can be what it is in Pirandello's *Henry IV*, the victory of life over the man's will to permanence, the man's betrayal by that very life that had made him what he was and what he willed to remain.

All these definitions and images are at bottom a description of a defeat of life, a defeat of the human inner life trying to find itself and its due form. In all tragedies we see the conflict of wills; we see elements of human life that are set against one another, both good in so far as they are alive, but one by its disproportionate amount destroying the other. In one of the greatest tragedies this failure extends even to the drama itself. A part of the universal melancholy of Shakespeare's play consists in the fact that the dramatist never succeeded in finding a dramatic form that could completely express his idea; even as a play *Hamlet* expresses tragic defeat.

Aristotle speaks of tragedy as dealing with superior persons. We could not say that in our modern drama, but we can say that tragedy deals with elements of living that are superior because *they are more intense*. Comedy exhibits a less intense life but sets it against a scale of social values by which individual desire or excess may appear disproportionate and hence ridiculous. Both comedy and tragedy might be included in the gift of a great dramatic poet, as Plato in the *Symposium* says by way of his Socrates, who forces Aristophanes and Agathon to admit, much against their

Greek inclinations, that a great tragic power in a poet ought to include the comic. Humor in social comedies is measured in its importance by the extent to which it becomes revealing. The lowest form of humor in comedy is the joke, the pun, the witticism stuck in for its own sake and put into the mouths of any character regardless. Of these are the wisecracks of Broadway and the epigrams of Oscar Wilde. Next comes the piece of humor that is comic in itself but much more so because of its comment on the character that says it. Sheridan's Sir Anthony Absolute abounds in such humor. The highest form of humor is that which finds expression in all the terms of the comedy, in the character, the action, and the place in the play's design at which it occurs. Of these, George Kelly has a fine instance in his *Torch Bearers* when in a midst of a performance by a group of stage-struck amateurs in a provincial town, the young widow whose husband's death had prevented her playing the leading rôle, cannot keep from behind the scenes and when the curtain calls are taken, cannot resist but goes on, mourning veil and all, and takes a bow. This is funny itself, it shows the woman's nature and her relation to the comic theme; and, coming where it does in the play, it sums up the whole folly that is being held up for laughter. In *Tartuffe*, the spot at which Orgon's mother refuses to believe ill of the hypocrite even after he has been exposed, is perfect comic detail. It reveals the old woman's inmost self; it comments on hypocrisy and what that works in people's minds; and at this stage of the plot it shows Orgon himself what he was like at the beginning.

The technical charm of a good comedy of manners

can be likened to modeling in relief, where the limits are fixed and where within a depth of an inch the values are caught and the implications achieved. In that finest scene in any English comedy of manners, that in which Congreve's Millamant consents to marry Mirabell, the dazzling quality of the writing derives from the fact that within their limits of banter and epigram Congreve has given us the sense of two noble natures, of true passion, of intense concern, without ever losing for a second his scale, his touch, his airy key; with the waving of a fan he manages to imply the winds that blow through the vast world of life.

In romantic comedy at its best that "swift perception of similarities" which we call wit takes on yet happier revelations. It becomes incandescent; the similarities extend into felicitous imagination, we have poetic comedy, wings that fly out of the window of the social drawing room, songs that forget the limits of a sane society. Lower down the scale comes ordinary romantic comedy, the sentimental humor with which we are familiar. The essence of all romantic comedy high and low is its freedom from that more exact measure by which social comedy gets its values. The essence of the romantic is possibility, the liberty of adorable escape.

To call a play a farce is nothing against it. Some of the best comic dramas are farces. Bernard Shaw often writes what is at bottom brilliant cerebral farce, and Pirandello's theatre is farce or, to be more exact, is *commedia dell' arte* in which the familiar characters are ideas, as abstract and unreal as Harlequin or Columbine, with the brain as the public square where their lively actions take place. One of the traits of farce and melodrama—which parallels farce—is exaggeration, as everyone knows, the heightening beyond probability or possibility that each may employ when it chooses. But this exaggeration is only a phase of what is their essential difference from comedy and tragedy, which is their freedom from the stricter conditions. Their flight is reckless, they are the playwright's trip to the moon. Farce is free to disregard those limits within which the sweet sanity and humor of comedy appear. Melodrama is free to avoid the tragic finality, to evade its conclusion. Farce is closer than comedy is to tragedy because of its stretch beyond the bounds of a social measure and good sense. Melodrama is closer to comedy than tragedy is because it need bother with the final truth only so much as it chooses. Both farce and melodrama take the cash and let the credit go; they eat their cake and have it too. Through this they are lower forms of drama.

Alongside these dramatic forms runs the perennial drama of sentiment, plays that fall under almost any head so long as it is not disagreeably important. The abilities, as Goldsmith said, that can hammer out a novel are fully sufficient for a sentimental play. You need "only to raise the characters a little," give "the hero a riband," the heroine a title, and "mighty good hearts" to them, with a pathetic scene or two, and a new set of scenery. For these dramas we may remember the French proverb for actors—*pour les sots acteurs Dieu créa les sots spectateurs*—and say that for simple-minded art God made simple-minded occasions.

There is one point we recognize too little about all dramas, whether tragedy, comedy, farce or melodrama. This is the truth of structure, by which I mean the degree to which the structure of a drama is a part of its idea, as the height of a table is a part of its truth; I mean that in drama, structure and tone are, as they are in music and architecture, expressive elements. In a drama there is a certain final expression that lies in the sheer order of its development, in its proportions, in the emphasis of its parts. The exact spot in *Macbeth* at which Fleance escapes, the spot at which is sprung the ironic surprise of the last of the witches' prophecies and thereafter the ensuing speed of the exposition and of the dénouement, all establish a large part of what Shakespeare desires to express. Goldoni's comedy of *La Locandiera*, usually spoken of by criticisms in English as very slight, takes its admirable depth most of all from the sequence of its parts, the order in which it progresses, the fine, sane, sweet and witty openness of its development by which its relationships and parts are assembled like the parts in a sunlit landscape.

The superiority of Molière over all other writers of comedy consists not in any words or single character so much as in his tone. The greatness of Molière's plays lies in their tone. His tone appears not so much in anything said or done in the course of a play, and not so much in the characters created, as in the distribution of accents, the sequence of parts and the management by which Molière makes things more or less insignificant and obvious in themselves say something significant when set together; he contrives an order and combination that will itself help to express his idea. Many a drama from the Latin mind, from the French or Italian or Spanish, is lost to us on just this basis; we cannot judge it because so much of it is expressed in its structural proportion and tone, and these are not always easily perceived by us. On one hand we find in them no mention of God, aspiration or soul, none of that conscientious perturbation, vagueness or solemn concern that gives us the impression of profundity or seriousness. On the other we understand nothing of what is said through the structure and tone; and so we grant the author's vivacity but deny his depth.

WHEN IS IT A PLAY?

How MANY times have we heard that a play was interesting but not a play of course, that a statue was good but not sculpture, a building effective but not architecture! It is the kind of thing that people say who prefer to see themselves as talking sense rather than talking what they like because they like it and finding out artistic principles later. This business of not being a play was said of Shaw when he began, of Chekhov, Brieux, and others. It is the sort of thing that has always been said and always will be.

A piece of writing intended for the theatre may be indeed interesting but not for all that a play. Or it may be a play but a very bad one. But if, interesting or uninteresting, it fails to be a play, it will not fail to be so from any cause that the aesthetic reasoners intend. For the most part they are talking nonsense.

They listen to a piece acted in the theatre. It moves or entertains them, they admit that, but they have something in their minds which prevents its passing for a play. This something amounts to a conviction that there is some special way in which a play to be a play must be written, some group of patterns or some formula on which a play is to be built. According to their schools or prejudice they lay down principles and rules.

The hole in the argument appears at once. Who is to say what the formula, the standard, is to be? It is plain that the ways of writing a drama have changed; Sophocles to Shakespeare—Shakespeare to Ibsen—could anything be further apart in a score of outer qualities? On this basis we should never get anywhere with the question. Every new sort of writing that is brought to the theatre, in the sense that Shaw brought something new, or Pirandello, will open up at once the old dispute; and only by personal endorsement of this or that formula can anything be decided as to the piece's being a play, though meanwhile perhaps the public goes on crowding to see it. It fares well, it draws crowds, but it is not a play. Something is clearly wrong.

The proof of the pudding is in the eating. Which means that it is a pudding so far as it goes down pleasantly and nourishes us. So with a play. A play is a piece of literature about a section of life written in such a way that it will go over the footlights, in such a way that what it has to say it can say in the theatre. That is the sole test. If it can do this it is a play, good or bad. It is a play in so far as the idea, the content, of it is expressed in theatre terms—the space relationships, the time elements, the oral values, the personal medium of the actors, and so on—as distinguished from the terms of literature.

Poetry or art, as Plato says, is a general name signifying that process by which something is where something was not before. We may say that the something that has arrived consists of a form and an idea; the idea was never born till it had the form to express it, the form never existed without the idea to determine it. An idea, whatever other form of existence it may have, does not exist in the theatre until it achieves a theatrical body. A play can exist only in theatre terms. The question as to whether a play is a play or not rests, as that question in every art does, not on rules or standards but on one fundamental basis. That basis is the relation between the idea and the medium.

Is it possible to have a piece of writing, of dialogue, of direct discourse, that will be dramatic and yet not a play? Yes. That means that it is not in terms of the theatre; it is dramatic without being theatrical. The look in two people's eyes may be dramatic at a certain moment and yet not be such that you could see it four feet off, much less from the audience; and so it is not theatre.

But before we say that, we want to be sure to ask ourselves a very pertinent question: What theatre is it that these discourses or these expressions like the look in two people's eyes, fail to be? In terms of what theatre do they fail to be said? The theatre may be dilated in such a manner that dramas not at the moment possible may find in time a theatre that can express them. In music, for example, the orchestra makes possible ideas not expressible on the Egyptian pipes and strings. An audience may someday in the future arrive to whom certain qualities may be perceptible and exciting that in this age we cannot convey to our audiences. Audiences now understand and respond to Freudian ideas and Bergson conceptions that would have bored or puzzled the public who went to see Booth and Forrest. What is impossible in one theatre and for one audience may under other conditions and for another audience be good theatrical matter.

We have arrived at a point where we seem to be agreeing that stageability is all that is needed to have a play. And this is true in a sense. But what of the play that is worth-while? When does this—to use Mr. O. W. Firkins's admirable phrase—"flowing vagueness" of the stageable cease to be worthless and become of worth? It may be only trash. What will make it take on value and significance? Are we driven back after all to the formula?

The answer is No, not to any given formulas. Certain general canons and forms have been found to serve in the case of certain kinds of dramatic matter; Aristotle, for example, could establish certain rules for Greek tragedy, rules excellent for dramas that are close to the ideas of Sophocles, though less so for Euripides, some of whose plays fail because of the fact that he could neither use the form available for him to express his matter fully and inevitably on one hand nor, on the other, to trim and alter his matter to suit such form. We are driven back not to any formula but to the principle that underlies every formula when it arrives at its full expressiveness, and therefore at the point where it is most fully alive. This principle is that within every content, worthless or notable, is implied its form. In any art great matter may be indicated, but it is not expressed until in its own kind there is created a form for it. This form illustrates certain principles and contains its formula no doubt. But when we come to any other work of art, this formula applies only in so far as the two works share the same quality or idea, otherwise it has no point.

You cannot say, then, for example, that such and
such is not a play because it violates the unities or is
in one long act or has a speech of ten pages' length.
But you can say, for example, that when a dramatist—
as I remember to have seen once in a manuscript—
writes that the heroine turns and walks to the door at
the back of the room and as she reaches it smiles a
radiant, happy smile, he may be writing fiction but is
not writing in theatre terms, since the audience could
not see at all the smile, which therefore as theatre it
does not exist. You can say that in his good moments
Bernard Shaw writing a sentence of thirty lines, three
hundred words, is still writing theatre, because by
means of the steady progression of its parts, by means
of its balances and phrases and words, and the click of
its thinking, the sentence achieves what will make it
speak over the footlights and live in the theatre,
whereas many a shorter sentence in other writers
would spell despair to the actors and to the audience
flat apathy.

❧ 7 ☙

NEW MATTER

WHEN A NEW figure, a man like Shaw or Pirandello or Eugene O'Neill, appears in the theatre with a new work to exist beside the works that we already have, we agree to attack him. Consciously or unconsciously we put him through his trial. We fly at him as fowls would at a newcomer in the barnyard; we try to spur and peck, to crack his head.

The newcomer, however, although he is different, a different shape, with different ways, is a fowl like the rest, and in time his existence will be admitted. The new play is a play, its idea proves itself in the theatre, restated in theatrical terms it comes over the footlights alive to the audience. Such a play is an important arrival, new in both form and content, since nothing in art can be new without being new in both form and content. Its idea, then, has been expressed, its soul has found a body, its content a form. In it appears a piece of creation successful because unified throughout; and through this unity we discern the essential character by which it is different from every other theatrical work. It takes its place, then, in the theatre, sometimes after great delay because of its diversity or suddenness; it will survive its epoch a longer or shorter time according to its significance, or according to its fortune

—which after all at times is mere chance. And yet in the nature of things we were right to attack it, to try to bar its place, since in life all birth is attended by struggle and contending forces.

But there is now and again a newcomer in the theatre who never quite becomes a part of it. His play is new because the idea in it is new; it is not wholly theatre because the artist has not got it expressed in theatrical terms throughout, or at least not to an extent that will carry it over the footlights.

A work of D'Annunzio's like *The Dream of an Autumn Sunset* would be a perfect instance, and his *Dream of a Spring Morning*. These pieces are plainly not theatre. Their ideas are luminous and beautiful and rich; but not in the characters nor the incident nor the style itself, not in the structure nor the kind of heightening employed, is there what will lend itself to expression in the terms of the theatre, what will survive the conditions that we know as theatrical, the conditions of space, the *optique du théâtre*, of the immediate presence of the actors, of special time values, sound values, and the rest. That D'Annunzio's two pieces are beautiful writing in verse and in dialogue, are poetic literature, is certain; but nobody would pretend that they are created in terms of the theatre, even a theatre of pure declamation, if such a one existed.

Confronted with such a piece as one of these, when it is freshly arrived in the theatre, we agree to attack it also, as we did Shaw and Pirandello. This time with more assurance we resist, for the theatrical weakness of the piece makes its cause weaker either to combat or to neglect.

Meantime we go with pleasure and approval to a

play of Molnar's or a piece like Bernstein's *The Thief*. Both we speak of as plays that are able if not great, as good theatre writing, as admirable craft. These playwrights know their business. They are not important as figures in the modern drama; they have no great deal to say, they are not significant artists, but both can write good, working plays.

The question can be raised, then, which of these two sorts of writers in the theatre is most important? On one hand we have a poet with his idea, trying to express it in theatre terms, trying to find a theatrical body for it, and failing for the major part or failing almost wholly. On the other side we have a skillful craftsman, with an idea that he can see as effective theatrical material; with no particular bias or urge of his own; willing to oblige, to trim his sails, to shape the idea to some workable, salable, entertaining form that will go expertly over the footlights? What in each of these is more valuable in the theatre or how does each in his own way serve?

It is the man with the idea, the poet, however incomplete as a dramatist, who is more important.

Plays like Mr. Galsworthy's *Skin Game* and *Loyalties*, either of which is at bottom a thesis presumed but only chattered about in words and carried over the footlights on an arbitrary dramatic frame, have their place and value to the theatre. Such plays supply entertainment, they keep up the technical machine of playwriting, they keep alive what we might call a kind of technical body in the art. At the same time they obstruct new forms, and thus prevent or distort new contents that need a new form to express them. But that is in the course of all nature, and is only another instance of that force in all created shapes that tends to hold them together as opposed to the force that tends to break them down.

That such plays are often only empty masks over a stale or lifeless content is obvious. A true artist not yet arrived at successful creation may well despise them, while envying perhaps their success in the world. Their security, slightness and willingness to please only puzzle and enrage him, for his own urge and travail leave him no such pleasant traits. They are also further proofs to him of the fact that the second-rate, the imitation, the borrowed and mollified, in art has always—as Eugene O'Neill said to me once—a better chance of immediate success than the best ever has.

But for audiences these plays have a genuine appeal. They are first of all entertaining, which any work of art ought to be—our instinct tells us that. And such plays have a knack of proposing a real idea or problem and getting the livelier juices out of it without really going into it at all. We get the sense that we are present at a deep discussion; in reality we have only a deep question raised and scarcely touched. The play touches it only in spots or evades it quite; you can find fifty plays on the same pattern as the one immediately on hand, but they express fifty different ideas, one form for fifty ideas! The effect of such a play is flattering because of the high matter proposed, and is comfortable because no high response is really exacted of us. We appear to get the distinction without the pain, the prestige without the cost.

Such dramas, however, it must be said, are by no means to be despised. They are good bad plays. They constitute the main body of the respectably important theatre. And when a significant artist does come along, a man trying to find for his content a body that will express it, that will be inseparable from it, he has in them ready to his hand a technical substance, a medium, in which to begin. According to his nature and idea, he will tear it, fight it, cursing and defying it with his lofty enthusiasm and divine intolerance. At best, perhaps he will even grant to its practitioner a moderate excellence, on the recipe of the Greek epigrammatist who said, "All Cilicians are bad men save only Cinyras, he alone is good, and Cinyras is a Cilician." Or he will twist it or fill it out and carry it to a fresh completion parallel to the high moment in its history when it was a significant body for a significant soul. Ibsen did just that with the general dramatic formula of Scribe and Augier when they after a fashion paralleled Molière, in whom the general prose method that he employed had found a summit. To wish all this middle level in the arts destroyed and thrown into the sea, as Tolstoi did, is individual, essentially barbarous, and unsocial. This artistic middle level constitutes a society in art, a general social system and scheme. It is wholesome for the life of the theatre as a social system is wholesome for men. And within it in the same way arises the individual, to struggle against it, understand it, transcend it, and express himself in its terms and it in his.

But when all is said and done the poet is more important in the theatre than any of these competent playwrights who say little but speak so expertly and so well. The reason for this touches on the nature of art and its ways of life.

The energy or stream of life by which creation

arises, a discovery of bodies that will contain and express it, goes on and on. Within it are the two principles, one of which seeks always to discover its due form and to maintain it, and the other which tends to break down this form. This expresses the very essence of what is living, of the fire that in due time "on the ashes of its youth doth lie, consumed with that which it was nourished by." This is what Euripides meant by his God Dionysos, whose body could not be bound by chains or the prison cell, and whose radiant life drew men to their release, glory or destruction.

When in art the life departs from the form, it is left as only a dead fact, a mask that once expressed some reality within. If this work is repeated nevertheless, and goes on being made to serve, despite its inexpressiveness, despite its emptiness, we have only husks, old lumber or else machines, pieces of contrivance that have been found to work up to a point at least. They do not express what they once expressed nor do they express what they assume now to express, though they may be up to a point effective and may still more or less work.

But in the history of ideas, morals, life, art, what counts is not these forms once expressive and not yet fallen from their vital estate. What counts is not, for example, an idea, a mental form, once understood by being alive and now barren but endorsed by tradition; or an arbitrary morality without spiritual pressure; or a suffocating tragedy like Addison's *Cato,* in the Greek pattern, or Eugene Walter's *Paid in Full* with Ibsen's form taken over, or Noel Coward's play where the mask of Ibsen's *Ghosts* is used to contain the facile trash of *The Vortex.* What counts is this force of life as it goes discovering, creating, and fulfilling the forms that reveal and express it. By this a work of art is alive.

This does not mean to imply some progress or evolution toward perfection in the art of the theatre as the centuries and epochs pass. We are not discussing progress or improvement. It merely means to describe the process by which in every age works of art have arrived, great or small, but whole, unified in themselves, a form and content one and indivisible.

It follows, then, that the supreme thing in the theatre is the arrival of a work of art in which we perceive that an idea has found a theatrical body to bring it into existence. The more significant the idea the more significant the work of art. But next in importance after this complete achievement comes the idea, the living content.

The poet, then, the maker of life, coming into the theatre—even though he cannot wholly express his content in theatrical terms but leaves it only an incomplete experiment in the theatre or perhaps only a piece of literature—can add to the theatre's content. I am not saying that his aim is high, that his reach should exceed his grasp or any such well-meaning platitude. The point is that his substance is alive, and through his poetic light, is luminous.

It may be that he will get his matter said but partially. But having it to say and straining at the theatrical medium to get it said, he may dilate the whole region of the art. He stretches the theatre's capacity for expression. Some later comer may be able to carry farther toward perfection what he has broken ground for. The first spirit may prepare the way and make more free of outer obstacles and inward inhibitions the course of a great artist that follows, as Sydney and the first poets of England's Renaissance did for Spenser, as he and Marlowe did for Shakespeare. Or some second-rater may, by trimming the edges of his content and by being amiable about the expression he gives to it, make it a part of the theatre's matter, as Pinero carried Ibsen into the English theatre. One play like Eugene O'Neill's *The Hairy Ape*, though it may not succeed completely in getting into theatrical form his whole idea, is worth to the theatre a thousand *Thiefs*, *Loyalties*, and *Other Dangers*, however expert they may be.

We may have a hundred good craftsmen in the theatre to one poet. They are at home in life and it costs them little. The poet pays as he goes. They see what they do, and it may be good as far as it goes. The poet may or may not always see but he knows that his eyes are alive.

What is true of the dramatist and drama is in its own way true of artists in the other arts of the theatre and of these arts, and any discussion of new substance provides a comment on Little Theatres, amateur theatres that is. There are too many of these groups and organizations of late years to be overlooked. What harm and what good they do to the theatre art has become an issue with a hot debate to it.

In the first place Little Theatres by their very natures and *raison-d'être* are more hospitable in their attitude toward departures and new forms in drama than the regular theatre is likely to be, and they risk less than the commercial venture, so that what the commercial theatre will not even consider is freely welcomed by them. But this is obvious; it is with re-

gard to production, acting or décor that they will bear
discussion.

These amateurs, militant sometimes and self-confi-
dent, help the theatre by stretching its range, bringing
into it new ideas. They experiment, they have courage
and at times genuine vision toward the art's future. To
their acting they may bring conviction and a kind of
raw faith. They are unspoiled by a mechanical craft
that is ready to hand for all effects, and so by the sheer
bona fide response that they give to a play they ex-
plode themselves into a rendering of it that a sophisticated actor with his ready-made craft could never
attain; they and their acting are closer to the play than
such an actor could ever be. They, in sum, by this
freedom and good faith, help to discover an acting
form for the play's content. At times their very ignorance or lack of training leads them to methods not
intended but really worth-while and to effects that are
moving though not foreseen. They reap a certain excellence from their defects. In production it is the
same. The mere lack of traditional method and professional attack may be at times a sort of freedom;
which, combined with the crusading will and the enthusiasm of exploration into fresh regions, may lead to
fine results. In décor the very poverty of money and
material or the limitation in stage space and equipment
may, if there be talent too and fresh inspiration, lead
the way toward a new economy and excellence in
theatrical design.

If these are the benefits, and benefits too valuable to
be lost, to the theatre art that such groups and organizations can do, there are harms also.

Such amateur groups may hurt the theatre by supplying examples of talk and theory rather than actual expression. They are likely to be full of people who have ideas and have theories of how things should be done, but who cannot do them. In acting, for example, such people may have a conception which they can attempt on the stage and even at times indicate to the audience, without any power to project it, to bring it alive in terms of acting, to make it engaging in such a way that the audience comes back at it with lively response and entertainment and not with mere dutiful appreciation and a patient endurance of good intentions.

Too often, too, and most unfortunately such workers feel unduly superior to the commercial theatre. They talk too freely about "hokum," by which they mean familiar tricks and the good old stand-by devices that the theatre works for its ends, but at the same time they have not enough realized that it is the vitality and reality put into a thing you do rather than its past history that counts. They are too apt to fancy that the professional theatre is to be despised somehow for wanting to please and even to make money, though these are perfectly natural inclinations, and when it comes to the point not always despised by the most exalted enterprises. Such amateur devotees tend toward much too wholesale a scorn for the established or successful. Such an amateur worker may scorn David Belasco's trimming his sails to the wind of public fads, if you like, and maintain, or shout, that his ideas are never distinguished or deep or bold in spirit. But for him to pitch overboard all the technical resource, tireless effort, canny sense of the audience and the labor or talent for the revision and pointing up of effects, that he has observed in such a theatrical craftsman as Belasco, is pathetically absurd and more or less fatal. In painting, no idea in itself that may be in your head could make you superior to Bougereau; however you may despise him, Bougereau at least could express to the last expertness what he had to express, but your great idea, unless you can paint at least some of it, has nothing to do with painting at all and only messes up both the canvas and the argument.

Finally the amateur has done and goes on doing our theatre much harm by this contribution toward the breaking down of the line that separates it as an art and a profession from something that anybody might do at will. The modern theatre is full of people, who, one way or another, arrive now and then without learning their business, arrive by personality alone, or personality garnished with a slight talent or propelled by a strong current of raw theatrical power, or blessed with some accident of publicity or moneyed patron, or a dozen other of those chances that are open to us in our romantic American chaos and riches and abundance of all sorts. To these hit and miss successes we must add the crowds of untrained dreamers, job seekers, and egoists that fill our theatres and lower its technical level, confuse art with society and reduce a bright and difficult region to mediocrity and mere private chance. You do the theatre, or any art, great injury when you lead the public to think that anyone is suited to practice it who wills, that in it all men are born equal. This state of things has gone so far in our American theatre that much of it indeed could not be called professional, if, that is, we mean by a profession something that implies training or experience. Commercial is a better word, a great deal of our theatre is an industry like any other, employing persons and personalities. This the amateur can scarcely hurt. But we can blame him at least for some share in bringing it about.

And yet these amateur theatres cannot be spared. They may break ground for us, and set up a balance to the merely commercial. In the professional they challenge the old methods and the craft that settles into barren mechanics. They remind the theatre art of the cost of all growth, the agony of new vision and new birth, and that it too perhaps must lose its life to find it. And most of all they, in the absence of technical craft, drive the artist back to the source of all his art, which is in himself, his quality, intensity, and idea; and remind all of us that the kingdom of heaven is within us.*

* The immense extension of theatre enterprises, in what we call Off-Broadway theatres, summer companies with visiting stars, and theatres in the universities and cities is one of the most notable developments of recent years. Many of them are in no sense amateur.

◄§ 8 §►

REVIVALS OF PLAYS

PLAYS OFTEN survive their epoch, which is to say they go on being significant as an expression of life. But conditions may have changed meanwhile, the theatre where they must be played may be different, the conceptions that the audience brings to the theatre are different. How to revive the play becomes a problem.

There are numerous theories about the revival of plays. Take a work of Shakespeare's, *Macbeth*, for example. According to one theory *Macbeth* should be revived exactly as Shakespeare made it and as it was produced in his own time. Everyone knows this theory from various experiments in what is called Elizabethan production. We have all experienced these occasions or often read of them: the apron stage, the double-storied alcove, the scenes unchanged, the branch for the forest, the placard for a street in Verona, the audience on the stage, and so on and on, according to the producer's scholarship or sense of the picturesque. This we are to assume is the only way in which the values in Shakespearean drama can be achieved.

The answers to this theory are several. In the first place we do not know exactly how the play was given in Shakespeare's time.* In the second place if we did know just how the play was given, and reproduced *Macbeth* exactly as it was when King James saw it, our audience would not understand it, not even in the matter of pronunciation, not to speak of tempo and the stage arrangements and stage conventions. In the third place even if the audience understood, the play would mean something different from what it once meant, in the same sense that a remark of Caesar's separated by centuries and continents cannot say to us quite what Brutus and Pompey took it to say.

In the fourth place, and finally, there is no lasting state to anything, no is-ness in life by which we can settle something once and for all and have it stay put. The sum of an idea consists in a set of relationships; its

---

* Mr. Leslie Hotson in his volume, *The First Night of Twelfth Night* (London, Rupert Hart-Davis, 1954), gives an absorbing account of the performance of the play at Whitehall Palace, Twelfth Night, 1601-02. The book is heavily documented from court lists, letters and reports from many persons who were guests or spectators or otherwise involved. It proposes a radical departure indeed from the generally accepted tradition as to theatres and the performance of plays in the Elizabethan period. The halls and theatres where plays were given had seats all round, known as "degrees" for spectators. There was no back curtain or wall; the play was acted openly in the middle of the floor. An arena . . . "A wooden O." There were small units of frame and canvas, known as *mansions* or houses, painted to represent buildings of various types, as required by the play to be given, with practical doors or curtains to be drawn away to reveal some action within. The *houses* were to represent all the clearly marked localities; they were set up before the performance began. Many records and writings of the time describe these stage settings as much richer and finer than they have often been thought to be. The position of the stage was in the middle of the hall. This method of the "circle" for plays was in use till 1665, when Charles II ordered a change to the modern proscenium arch, drop curtain, and background of movable scenery for legitimate drama.

truth arises from the relation existing among its diverse elements. It is obvious, to take some examples, that in the costume of a man whom we must portray as moderate, a hat that would be immoderately small in Siena might be moderate in every way in London, or vice versa; that an axiom about decency might apply most to bodily functions in one era and to social fitness in another; or that what was once manly may have become now only brutal or effete. This is true in the moral and intellectual life and it is true in drama. We have the idea, we have the dramatic elements into which it will go. Of these elements the drama is one, the stage conditions another, the conceptions of the audience another and so on. A play is a piece of writing in which the idea has found a theatrical body for itself. The rightness of this theatrical body derives from the relations among its elements. But with the passage of time comes a change in certain elements; to produce the play again the relationship among them must be again discovered. To keep the play alive we must find always anew a body to express this idea. In sum we must translate it into the medium of the moment; we must discover afresh for it the right mental and visual accents, or it will be dead, an empty mask that no longer contains the life that is there to be expressed.

In *Macbeth* Shakespeare took a story full of the fierce, primitive lust for living, full of haunted moors and the ancient, evil powers of the earth, and gave to it the rich texture of the seventeenth century. To another age than Shakespeare's the fullness of this seventeenth century quality might seem to dim the glare of this older and more primitive quality, quite as a baroque ornament set in a Georgian room might express more brightness and complexity than was intended by it. To yet another age the primitive element in *Macbeth* might express a greater degree of barbarism than Shakespeare meant. In every case, as must be obvious, this drama of *Macbeth* must be restated in the terms of the moment if what is its essential truth is to be given a living theatrical body. To do otherwise may be interesting as archaeology, obstinate as academic statistics, quaint as folklore, but in the meantime the necessary life of the play, its essential content, must suffer or be lost.

If, then, the fundamental problem in every revival of a play is how to restate it in such a way as to keep alive its characteristic idea, what shall we say of the type of revival that violates the quality of the play, of Mr. Robert Edmond Jones' and Mr. Arthur Hopkins' revival of *Macbeth* for instance, so memorable, prophetic and profound? Well, that too is art. It differs from the intention of which I have been speaking in this respect: it does not aim to express the complete essential nature of the play, it uses the play to express some idea that the producer wishes to express, as Liszt might do with an air of Shubert's or as Michelangelo did with a classic motive in architecture. This is virtuosity sometimes, like some of Liszt's compositions, or it is a sort of creation in which the artist takes the play as a theme or material from which to project his own special creation, as Shakespeare himself may have taken an old play of *Macbeth* and used it to his own ends. In revivals of plays, such a method is justified by its success, by the significance of what it creates. A dozen such violations of *Macbeth* might enlarge in twelve respects the scope and meaning of the play for us and so dilate its region. In such a method the artist-producer proceeds by his own imagination and at his own peril, his result may be luminous and beautiful or asinine and quite awry.

One thing in every revival of a play must above all come first. This is that you know what your idea is which you either derive from the play or will employ the play to express. To return to *Macbeth* as an example. The average producer of a Shakespearean play has neither culture nor acumen enough to arrive at a sum of what its quality or meaning is for him; he sees no one style to it; he merely gets along from one section of it to another, with hand to mouth conceptions, grasping at one quality or idea after another; which is why in most productions of his plays Shakespeare seems so made up of inspiration, fancy, confusion and mixed effects. The total idea that you may have of *Macbeth* cannot, of course, be fully expressed in words; it eludes mere words and awaits its own theatrical medium, as Beethoven's idea awaited its symphony. But—merely to glimpse the idea with a descriptive word—we may inquire if you wish to create primitive archaisms or baroque complexities or a sense of powers of evil, or what? What is it that you will try to create with this play as the material and with your theatre as the medium? That you must know. With this clear to you, you can set about finding a body for your idea; and, in so far as you can use your medium, you will achieve a unity, something that is alive, however satisfactory or not it may be to others, or significant in itself.

✥ 9 ✥

THE ACTOR

As ALL ACTORS who get anywhere at all know in their hearts, the actor is the liveliest part of the theatre. Modern invention may spread the visual side of the theatre in the moving pictures, the spoken side—perhaps soon the visual also—in the radio, and the theatre break up thus into its parts; but actors know that they remain the one element that can be had completely only in the theatre itself, and that they are necessary, therefore, to its very existence. Of all theatre elements they are closest to the audience. Of all theatre languages acting gets the readiest ear. The actors are the vehicle of expression on which most depends, and they know that their first business is to get themselves and their matter over the footlights to the audience, to turn all into theatre. They sense the fact that nothing counts except in relation to this theatricality. Probability in character, time, action, or likeness, naturalness or truth concern them only with regard to the theatre, to projecting what they create and to getting a response to it from the audience.

Actors sense the difference between acting talent and mere serious intention, they sense what a part sheer vitality and magnetism play in the actor's achievement. They know how audiences like spirit in an actor, well-adjusted egotism, engaging exhibition-ism, power, assurance, the impression of success—know how wise is the Spanish proverb that everyone likes the victor—*siempre es simpatico el que vince*. And they know that while the production of the play is being presented to the audience, they themselves are, of all the agents at work in this complex art, the chief, they are the protagonists. More than the designer's, who created the décor; or the dramatist's, who gave the play and the central theme; or the director's, who controlled and shaped the enterprise as a whole, their mystery and power are felt by the audience; they are the singers in the song. By instinct, intuition and talent, actors that are functioning in their art know these things, have all this straight. Whether they can explain them or not, these things exemplify the principles of their art. And audiences by the same intuition follow them freely.

We should not hold it against them, then, if actors often show how human they are by being frailty and innocence itself when they come to analysis and the-ory. Every one of us philosophizes over life to some extent at least, every actor does a little theory on his own. Then begins a confusion indeed, an aesthetic Babel, the ballad of the babes in the wood. Sometimes the actor's theory is a prattle of mere made-up expla-nations, like a man in the midst of a love affair trying to talk the psychology of sex. The actor will tell you, for example, that he has got to be natural, to be like life, when all the while what he is trying to do on the stage is not to represent a natural person or action but to present naturalness itself which is quite another thing; he tries to project into the audience what he thinks the natural is. He may tell you that he must keep to the truth, when there is in fact no truth of time, place or anything else that holds him except in relation to the effect he aims at, for he goes as fast or as slow as he likes, jumps his scenes over the earth, in the house one minute, the next on the sea, now speaking plain words, now bursting into song, now walking, now dancing.

Or he may be another sort of actor, one who is high up in ideas from an art theatre perhaps or a personage most regularly educated and strictly cultured before becoming an actor. He puts his brains to work upon the problems of his art. He talks, theorizes, paints too little with his brush and too much with his tongue, as Rodin said of Whistler, and so muddles up the whole question of the relation of his art to the theatre. He arrives at divers conclusions, according to his epoch, the group he runs with, or the teachers he has had. Actors, he concludes, perhaps, should be themselves. Acting is being natural. Or artifice is out-of-date and false. An actor should be the part he plays. Be sincere. There are a hundred theories; sometimes held by people who can only think, not act; sometimes talked by good actors who do the right thing and are only confused when they try abstractions and principles, who act like monarchs but talk like poor Poll. Some of them think straight, but most of them if they carried out the theories they announce would break their necks and the theatre's neck, or at least be far worse players than they are now. But this, as Cicero said of the early orators—before he arrived—is a horrid way of speaking— *asperum et horridum genus dicendi.*

Of all these theories the one actors suffer most from

lies in the naturalistic direction, and comes to them from the realistic drama. Compared to the actor, the dramatist, producer and designer are free; they can go forward toward new styles, can inject into the theatre their ideas, which the rest of the theatre can follow; the actor is the product of the theatre of his epoch. He does not point the way, he cannot quite begin a new style or method, for no matter what the theatre becomes, he is essentially a theatrical medium. He develops what is supplied him by the dramatist or producer, what their style is his style must be if he interprets for them. The main body of drama in our time has been realistic in method; and the acting of our time has developed out of that drama. And though a realistic actor may be great, just as a drama that employs realism may be great, the fact remains that realism is elusive; for the ordinary craftsman it is harder to achieve distinction when the sole requirement imposed upon him is to represent nature. Realism is the easiest method in which to miss style.

In the acting of our day one deadly principle has taken the lead: the actor should present to us the emotions he has experienced by putting himself in the character's place. This implies sincerity, naturalness and the rest of that familiar list of qualities, and might by twisting it be made to apply to acting of all kinds. But the danger of such a theory in most actors' hands is great. In naturalistic rôles an actor if he has the talent can go far on this basis of putting himself in the character's place and then expressing the emotion he feels in a given situation. Mr. David Warfield, for example, in *The Music Master* could by his imagination and dramatic sympathy put himself in the old man's place, could feel what he felt, and by his admirable craft could create all this for us. But when he tried Shylock that was another matter; his Shylock was a Ghetto father, with all the simplicity, intensity, fanaticism and pathos of his type. Mr. Warfield could give us what he might feel in Shylock's place and what he gave us was genuine and moving emotion. But the point is that he could not put himself in Shylock's place. He gave us what he felt as Shylock, but could not feel the Shylock of Shakespeare. He could not enter into this persecuted Jew in a seventeenth century fantasy, a character with his due ferocity and scars, but seen, nevertheless, through the perspective of a Venetian comedy written by a Renaissance poet. The trouble, obviously, with this theory is in its first term. Mere sincerity of intention does not necessarily put an actor into the character's place; nor does mere genuineness of emotion on the actor's part give us the right emotion for the character. After all, what we are interested in is the rôle, not in the actor's feeling natural.

There is no reason, however, why actors should be artists in words or artists in aesthetic theory. No doubt such a state of things would be most desirable, but we have no more right to demand such accomplishments of an actor than we have to ask Shakespeare to model the statue of Lucrece, or Mozart to write poems, so long, that is, as the actor has something to say in his own language, which is acting.

Acting is an art in which the artist uses himself, his body and voice, as a medium. The actor takes from a drama a person and the dramatist's comment on the person; he brings his inspiration and technique to the dramatist's imagination. This creation of the dramatist's he restates in terms of acting, bringing into existence a new creation that was not before. This creation of the actor's has then to be restated in relation to the whole play, the theme and the characters; it must be given its proper mask; and by this it becomes a part of another body, of the whole theatre work that is to be created.

Technical training and skill in his art develop and perfect the actor as a medium of theatrical expression, that is obvious. But there is an element about him that we may speak of as pure acting medium, which he has largely by birth, or to some extent by cultivation, and at his best by both.

We may speak of five aspects of this medium.

There is first—and most baffling of all when we seek explanations—the theatrical person, the player who goes vividly over the footlights. Some players click as they appear on the stage, we watch them because they in themselves seem to exist in theatre terms, as contrasted with good actors whose presence is interesting only by skill in their art or beauty or some pleasing personal quality. This theatricality is not to be confused with the popular *sex appeal*, an actor may not be conspicuously appealing in this way and yet may be theatrical, may project readily into theatre terms; just as some voices, good or bad, engage your ear at once. Indeed for the actor this personal theatricality corresponds to what a real singing voice—a voice whose life is at once contagious for the hearer—is to the singer, good or bad.

Second, there are the natural assets that the actor has for his business. This may be some great beauty of presence, or an effective body in shape and flexibility, or a good theatre mask, or all of these, down to a skin that takes the make-up well, an advantage in which, by the way, actors greatly vary.

A good theatre mask implies contours and conformations that can project themselves over the footlights into the theatre, eyes that can be seen, cheekbones that will not crowd them, teeth whose glitter carries a smile to the farthest row in the theatre, and so on. What one actor, though a profound artist, may succeed in creating only in the course of a long scene, another who is more or less a fool may establish the first minute he is on the stage merely because his brow has a noble outline, a splendid serenity upon it, or because the bone structure of his eye sockets, by throwing stage shadows over them or allowing room for black-leading, conveys the effect of tragic romance. A voice may express to its hearers a score of things that the speaker neither intends nor could understand. Such endowments as these are unescapable elements in the actor as a medium. They have not necessarily anything to do with soul, training or artistic intelligence; they are to the actor what his instrument, good, bad or indifferent, is to the violinist.

Third, there is the time-sense. One of the most expressive languages in the theatre is that of the time intervals. Actors with a sense of rhythm and an instinct for pause, cues and general tempo, can easily achieve sometimes what players who are much better artists reach only with arduous elaboration. Mr. Glenn Hunter, for example, who is a player without much imaginative scope, can often hit at once by means of his time-values what Mr. Morgan Farley, who has far more genuine artistic understanding but less acting gift, can approach only indirectly and laboriously.

Like the time-sense but in the region of the eye, is the actor's sense of movement and line. Here he transfers the time-sense into visual motion, whose rhythm, pattern and intervals become in themselves expressive as the rhythm in a ballad or a scherzo is expressive, as Michelangelo's design in line and mass is expressive in his *Campidoglio,* or as a spiral says a thing so very different from what an oval says. The flow of Charlie Chaplin's gesture and movement, for example, is unbroken and complete; Chaliapin in Boris exhibits a visual rhythm that is superb and superbly related to his own particular body and stature and wholly calculated in terms of them. Under this head falls the capacity for wearing costumes, which, in fact, come alive on the stage only through the wearer's sense of moving line.

This sense for the pure visual medium must not be confused with the gift of mimicry. Mimicry works through the medium of gesture of course but it turns on resemblance.

A mimetic gift in the actor corresponds to a good ear in the musician. It is a great advantage, but will not of itself make him an artist. Many good actors have little talent for mimicry. Mimicry is to acting what memory can be to culture and education, and like memory it must not be too easily despised. The imitation of others is an instinct born deep in us, and is the source of the actor's art. Acting is essentially based on men's actions as we see them in our daily experience; and an aptitude for imitating these actions may be taken as the first ready test of a man's born gift for this particular art.

In the theatre there is always to be found a sort of person, often intelligent enough, who can think, theorize and describe acting till we might mistake him for a player of some skill. The way to show such persons up at once is to let them imitate the simplest action of men and women and to see how certain they are to miss it flat. This gift for mimicry in the actor is like a gift for likeness in a painter. Such a knack will not make his drawing fine, but it will give him a kind of solid reality which he can begin with and which he can alter and force to his own ends. The painter, for example, takes the landscape as the material for the expression of his idea; it is plain that he can express his idea more adequately if he knows the exact appearance that he works from, and that we, on the other hand, by knowing just what he has done to this material know better what he has expressed. In order to translate a gesture into elegance or extravagance or drunkenness an actor may best begin by being able to reproduce the actual literal gesture that he sees in life. To that literal and basic gesture the shortest cut lies in the power of mimicry. All of which amounts to saying that it is from this actual, literal gesture and the knowledge of what it would be in any given case that all style evolves. The reason most of our extremely stylized productions seem so poor and misled is because the actors lack the needed style; and they miss this style because they do not command the simple, straight acting from which the style departs.

To these basic endowments and faculties in the actor we must add—as we must do, not only with the actor but with any artist—the rest of him, all that spiritual and mental and personal and peculiar sum that for want of a better word we should call himself. The sum of all, of himself plus his special acting gifts, is what the actor brings to his art, is what qualifies him as the medium of acting. He remains himself as pigment remains pigment in painting and in sculpture marble remains marble.

It follows therefore that the actor, being the medium that he works in as an artist, is never the character that he plays, or we should have no art. Even a Mr. Tom Jones acting himself on the stage would have to project in theatre terms his own notion of himself and his relation to the rest of the play. Even in such a case the actor cannot play from nature. He plays from an idea, which he sets up and which if you like he may have drawn from nature. He is Mr. Jones but the Mr. Jones projected into his acting is another matter. To say that another actor playing this part does not act Mr. Jones, he *is* Mr. Jones, makes such nonsense that it defeats itself. The actor is always himself, in every rôle he is himself. But he is himself only as a medium for his idea. He uses himself, his body, his voice, and the elusive personal quality that goes with these, exactly as Titian uses paint or Haydn sound, to create a form for his idea.

The relation of acting to emotion is an old problem in the art; the theories on the subject are many. Quintilian in the first century declared that the actor moves others only by being moved himself; which means that to make others weep you must first weep yourself. Diderot and Coquelin defended the famous paradox that you can be a great actor only on the condition of complete self-mastery and the ability to express feelings that are not felt, feelings, perhaps, even that you could not feel; by which last is meant that the actor can by a synthesis build up an image of emotions that are beyond his power to feel, that are ideal—as Greek sculptors created bodies beyond human perfection. These are the two extreme positions, and between them lie the various doctrines, theories and dogmas that would describe acting either as emotion once felt, at least, or imagined, and then translated into some expression in acting, which in turn is then to be repeated in performance after performance; or as inspiration, trusting to what comes at the moment on the stage; or as the warm heart and cool head that Joseph Jefferson spoke of, and so on and so on.

There could be no way of settling this timeworn argument. One man can experience an emotion repeatedly with more readiness than another; one has less need than another to feel the emotion at the moment in order to act it. There is another point also. Granted that an acting form has been found that will express the emotion and that the actor repeats when he wishes to express again this emotion, the fact remains that one actor may be more affected by the thing he does than another. By which I mean that he more than the other is excited by the acting that he does and is led back again by it to the emotion that it first arose from and expressed. Actors vary too in their strength of memory; one may have a better memory for form than the other, he can more readily recall just what he did when he first expressed the emotion; another may more easily remember the emotion itself and may on each occasion struggle anew for its expression. Actors, like artists in every art, vary in the extent to which their form or style, independent almost of whether it expresses a sincere emotion or not, is in itself engaging. In Mr. David Warfield's playing, for instance, for us to receive a marked sense of his craft would be distressing, since a certain genuine and natural conviction is a part of his effect; in Chaliapin the artist's style itself is exciting, some of his movements and vocal technicalities engage us, regardless of what is behind them, exactly as the play of Veronese's brush, or the sumptuous artifice of his figure arrangement, is a part of what his picture says to us.

All this may indeed be true, but there is one point at least that we must not be confused about, which is that we must never fall into the notion that emotion *per se* or any other reality in the player himself, makes acting; which finally depends on expression, and expression arrives only through the acting medium and technique. The fundamental principle in this debate over acting and emotion is that a form be found in terms of acting that will express to the audience a certain experience of the character. Acting may be bad for lack of the right form to express what is to be expressed, or because the form projected is empty of content, a sort of right form in the wrong place. But emotion with no projected form that will express it to the audience is not acting at all.

To create in this medium of himself the actor needs technique. Acting is a language in the theatre that must be learned. Without technique the actor cannot know the resources of rhythm, what tempo is, what the voice means to such ends as his, or how to recognize effects when he does get them, to retain from these what is most expressive and to repeat it when he wills. Through the avenue of technique the actor approaches all wit, elevation, variety and depth of style. Through his technique he establishes that firm outline that divides his creation from reality and heightens it into art. Without technique, however wonderful his own quality may be, he has no language to speak. Through technique he learns the use of his medium. Through technical labor he gets an intellectual discipline that helps to clarify his ideas; which in their turn are developed by this search for their right technical form.

If cultivation in his technique helps the actor's use of his medium, cultivation in general, a culture in thought, arts and living, will help his idea. Culture in other arts will nourish and promote the conceptions that he brings to his own. The technical qualities in one art can be transferred to another. You can take rhythm or emphasis, for example, and apply their expression in architecture to music or acting. The structure of Milton's style in *Samson Agonistes* is not unlike Michelangelo's in its formalism, pedantry, nobility and controlled but intense emotionalism. The rich texture of Veronese once it is felt and understood affords an approach to the texture of Shakespeare's writing. The phrasing in good music can throw light on the thought phrase and on word phrasing. I should think that Debussy would be the best guide to many a drama of Maeterlinck's, since the quality of their mood is so totally suggested in some of his music; and nothing, perhaps, could teach us more about acting Sheridan than the furniture and objets d'art of the period. An emotional or spiritual culture and exercise in one art enriches the substance that we bring to another. The dilation of his mental horizon by knowledge and ideas furthers the actor's opinion into sane judgment and his choice into distinction; it furthers too his understanding of the play and of his rôle in all its meanings and parts; the range, intensity and glamour of his own living cannot be divorced from the nature of his conceptions. The actor needs always to make of himself a material beautiful in quality and diverse in range for his art's sake; even the finest building is more beautiful for its marble's beauty.

Through the creation of his idea into acting form, the actor achieves a work of art, complete in itself and free of its material. If he has power behind the idea and the expression of it, he could, if he chose, do a beggar, not in whining rags but in the most exalted declamation and elegance. It will be an extreme case of unlikeness, and he will have to contend with the disappointment or resentment that we feel when we see what is a familiar fact so contradicted or distorted; he will have to convince us of the particular truth that he is expressing. Or he could take the reverse direction and do his beggar in shreds and patches. On the other hand he could do a king in robes and heroic speech, as in Aeschylus; or in homely cotton and the simplest realism, as in certain beautiful and moving folk dramas and rituals. The principle remains the same, which is the freedom and completeness of a work of art. The actor is as free of his material as any other artist. But the fact remains, nevertheless, that in acting this freedom is more dangerous, since acting of all arts rests most on imitation and arouses therefore more than any other art a strong demand for likeness. It happens too that the lively instinct for imitation born in us has us doing the stage characters inside ourselves before we know it; before we know it we are acting them, and so are doubly critical over resemblances and jealous of the facts of appearance and similarity.

But whether he works close to the surface of his material or remote from it, the actor must have one chief concern. Having made of himself an expressive medium, he must be concerned with his idea or conception. It is by that that he persuades toward himself the stream of life moving in others and that he becomes, like the beloved man in Bianor's poem, "lord of another's soul"—ψυχῆς κύριος ἀλλοτρίης. The poet when he speaks himself, Aristotle says, creates no image—in the same sense we may say that the actor when he is merely being himself is not an artist. Homer, he says, admirable as he is in every other respect is especially so in this, that he knows the part to be played by the poet himself in the poem. Only by his idea does the actor know his share in the whole work of theatre art that he serves; the rest of him is merely used by the director and the dramatist; it is mere medium like the paints, canvas and lighting.

ও 10 ৯৬

THE DIRECTOR

BEHIND EVERY production that we see in the theatre stands the director. He may be someone brought in to keep things from scattering all over the place, a sort of overseer and little else. He may be an ignoramus who gets a chance to be a boss, or an actor with a few tricks up his sleeve who is given charge over the company. He may be a fairly able fellow whose office is to get good curtains, keep the cues going and the stars to the front, or a fine artist who brings the theatre work into being, its parts justly related and its idea expressed. The importance or recognition of the director varies with various epochs. In the Attic theatre the archon oversaw the production of a play; the manager in the Elizabethan theatre bought, wrote, adapted and directed plays. In the modern theatre the director has been more signaled out and popularly recognized than ever before. There are people, even, to whom the director or *régisseur* seems the most important element in a theatrical occasion.

The director has the same relation to the theatre that the orchestra conductor has to music. He has no parallel in the other arts. He uses his actors as the conductor uses his musicians, and is related to the play as the conductor is to the score. The conductor is an artist, since he creates a musical body for the idea that he derives from the score. The director is an artist, good or bad, since he creates a theatrical body for the idea he has from the play. He is an artist or he is nothing.

Directors move more toward virtuosity when they take the play only as material for some idea that they wish to express. They are not concerned with giving us the play's idea so much as their own. An extreme virtuoso in the theatre uses the play as the other sort of director uses the actors or the décor, it does not provide the main idea or the mood of the theatre work but is employed to express his idea. He does not develop the play for what is in it but uses it to create a sort of drama of his own. He distorts the play and forces it to ends not its own but his. A familiar piece of virtuosity, so long known to so many that it no longer is seen to be such, is what is usually done to *The Merchant of Venice*. The seventeenth century comedy, with its light fable conceived in all the verve, vivid elaboration, brutality and lyricism of its time, is turned into the tragedy of a suffering Jew, and the leading actor in the part is directed to wring it dry for its last drop of pathos, race problem, social injustice and bitter edge.

A brilliant piece of virtuosity, frowned on by many, was the Hopkins-Jones production of *Macbeth*, where the Shakespearean substance of the play was distilled to an essence at once profound, haunting and macabre; and the drama and the scene that we saw on the stage seemed translated to our own viscera and the realms of our subconscious.

The line between extremes in directing should not be too sharply drawn. Most directing has in it streaks of more or less unintentional virtuosity that comes from a strong personal bias of the director toward the play. In general we may say that virtuosity sinks or swims by the significance of its idea. As a rule we rightly prefer the play's idea to some twist in a director's head.

The director that concerns us most tries to translate as closely as possible into the theatrical medium the idea or characteristic quality of the play he directs. He reads and responds to the play; in him the experience that the dramatist created in the play is re-created, he lives it again, he decides what its quality is to be, and with the means at hand sets out to express this quality. It is with regard to the play that this sort of director and the virtuoso differ from one another. With regard to the other elements in the theatre their problem is the same.

The capable director has three considerations that are most important in his use of the theatrical medium ready to hand.

First of all he must study his problem with his eyes on the use of all the elements involved. I mean this:

The director begins with the idea that he has deduced from the play he is to present in a theatre. He had as mediums through which this idea may be conveyed, the play, the acting, the décor, the stage movement. He must sense what in the idea will best be expressed in one medium, what in another, as one might know, for example, that a general mood is best expressed in music, a proverbial maxim in words, a concrete scene in painting. He must in sum before he goes very far with his more practical steps, with rehearsals and other proceedings, perceive what portion of the whole creation each of his mediums is to express.

He must consider how much, for example, of the burden of the occasion is to fall to the acting, in Gorki's *Lower Depths*—to take a good play—it is the individual characterizations, the ensemble and the mutual exchange among the actors, that must convey the idea to the audience; in *The Music Master*—to take a poor play—everything depends on the acting, on the pathos and sentiment that the actors create.

The director will consider, too, how much of the burden will fall to the dialogue itself. In Congreve's *The Way of the World*, for instance, the setting is nothing, a chamber not too bad is good enough, or even a curtain or someone's drawing room will do; what counts is the words, they count even more than the acting that follows them. Congreve's words are his main vehicle, and the dialogue is his director's main reliance. He will decide how much he will trust to the time-values in speech and action as the best element for the play's expression, remembering that just as the truth of a mile is its length, a part of the truth of a man's remark is its duration, and of two speeches is the time-interval between them. In most productions too little is said in these values and too much left to the lines and characters.

What is true of the time-values in directing is quite as true of the visual rhythm in the stage movement. In a play like Lenormand's *Les Ratés, The Failures,* each of the eleven scenes establishes a single action or event in the progress of the plot, and is very short, the dialogue concentrated; it needs therefore the fullest aid possible from other elements besides the lines and the gestures and the setting. In each scene so far as possible a certain pattern of movement needs to be created. This pattern stamps on our minds the relation of the characters to each other in what they are doing at the moment. For instance there is such a pattern inherent in the scene where the man comes in drunk. He staggers from the door to the chair opposite, the woman from her bed by the door comes to him, she leans over him as he talks, she kneels to undo his shoes, at the sight of his degradation she drops her head on his knees. There is one line of movement, one single pattern that expresses the scene's idea, the idea of his ruin, of her love and grief folded like wings around him. In the cathedral scene where the man confesses his infidelity to the woman, the two of them, when the rest of the company have filed out, remain seated together at the base of a column and in the midst of the vast spaces of the darkening church. By this design in stage position they seem bound together, small, defeated, pitiful; and what happens to them seems to pour from the two of them there and down on them. In a scene from one of Charlie Chaplin's films his movement establishes a flowing line from start to finish and much of what remains in our minds is the pattern of it.

The director can consider how much of the content of a theatre work will most fully appear in atmosphere and design, how much, that is, he will depend for his effects on the décor provided the play. The right setting for the second act of Mr. Shaw's *Caesar and Cleopatra*, for example, will be half the battle; that scene with the infinite desert by night, the shadowed, inscrutable, somber Sphinx, the rising moon that casts its immortal silver dusk over these and over the characters there, conveys to the audience the mood of time and power against which the ironic poetry of the lines will be true.

And finally the director must see all these theatre elements together, with what they express, and must relate them into a unity. There will be many avenues of expression all leading to the whole theatrical body created. The glory of the theatre is that it comes so close to human life that it breaks up into all our channels of response and expression; all are alive together and through all the whole sum appears. This insight into the revealing power of each of these theatre mediums amounts after all only to the director's being alive in it. Through these diverse avenues he seeks life for what he desires to create, exactly as in our daily experience we look at one thing and listen to another, or as we fling ourselves on words, on song, or color, on rhythm, action, ideas—sowing ourselves on every wind—in order to create ourselves in terms of living.

Within the nature of the play itself there is a problem for the director. He must see the play in its entirety, what aspect of it needs emphasis, what subordination, and what its main themes are and the sequence of its parts. *Othello*, for example, lives in its outline. The round pattern of the plot and of the leading characters is what expresses the idea, within this outline the shadings appear. Any detail or subjective stress that holds up the movement for a moment by just that much impedes the dramatic eloquence and sweep of the whole. Plays from Goldoni's or Molière's theatre, for instance, need strong outlining, the director must put the emphasis on the outline first of all, or the combinations and meanings of the play will be lost. A play like Chekhov's *The Three Sisters* needs a distributed monotony of emphasis, its quality is inward and atmospheric, and its idea appears in the diffused, not in the clear, boundaries of the thwarted plot. In *Tartuffe* the most intense stress should come in the third quarter of the play; the very last five minutes of it should have the same equable urbanity as the first five; the parallel in tone between these beginning and final intervals expresses the state of mind into which Molière wishes the play to settle—which is to say the tone. In *Ghosts* there are balancing emphases in the first act and the last. The most important thing about directing Goldoni's *The Fan* is to sustain the quick cues; it was largely for lack of this that the play failed of success when it was first produced, as Goldoni himself tells us.

There is another respect in which plays differ importantly and where the director's failure to see the point can distort a play or blur its effect. This turns on the relation of the lines and actions to the whole of the play. In Chekhov's plays, in *Ivanoff* for example, what the various persons do and say is highly characteristic of them; they are defined and expressed by what they say and do, and their words and actions in turn contribute to the plot and to the play's whole idea. In a play like Pirandello's *Così é, se vi pare*—It's so, if it seems so to you—many of the speeches could be said by any one of half a dozen characters; they do not relate to the particular character saying them so much as they do to the building up of the theme; they are like steps in an analysis. In the New York production of Pirandello's *Henry IV*, the expository scene spoken by the four pages failed of its dramatic function because of the actors' individualizing their speeches, making them, or trying to make them proceed from themselves. By this they lost the speed and continuity right for the scene; what we got was four people more or less expressing themselves on a point, where we should have gotten the effect of a point streaming through a brain, with the various arguments clashing and running against each other. The director needs always to study to know when a speech, or an action, is directly related to the play's plot or its whole idea; when it is related first to the character and through the character to the whole; and when it is much less related to the whole than it is to the character, of which it is a pleasing perhaps but arbitrary detail.

The director has next to consider his use of the actor, for the actor is his cardinal medium. On the acting hangs much of the play's immediate fortune.

To say, as some say, that the director must be an actor himself, that he must know how to do the thing he wishes the actor to do, is wrong. The conductor need not be able to play every instrument in his orchestra, as the architect who uses colored windows in his creation need not know how to paint glass. Obviously the director who is a good actor has a certain advantage, since he can show his company exactly what he wants them to do. But even that conclusion is not too final, and for three reasons: first, you can be a fine artist and have no gift at all for passing it on to another person; second, you can have a fine conception and technical knowledge to offer others, even though you yourself are without any gift for that lively creation that will make your idea into acting; and, finally, there is often a real advantage in giving an actor not something to be copied exactly but something that furnishes a lead, on which he can proceed to his own creation.

Directors vary in their use of actors. At one extreme is the director who lets the actor alone, does not say do it this way or that, but how would you do it? This method has certain merits. It freshens the acting by bringing into it more of the actor's own quality and own way of creation. It encourages his soul toward the expression of its own particular nature. It stiffens the dramatic texture by sharpening or leaving fresh the individual units whose contact or reactions make up the scene. The disadvantages are quite as obvious. Provided we have good actors and provided there are only two or three persons in the scene the result may be excellent, but good actors are not always to be had for the asking, and souls of depth and distinction are not universal, even in a democracy. Few plays consist of scene after scene with two or three characters in it. And even if we have such a play the whole of it needs its analysis and its right emphasis of parts, needs to be plotted out by an overseeing eye and to have this plot securely stated in the acting. For ensemble scenes, crowds, masses, groups, this method is worthless.

Of this general method in the use of actors, though not at the extreme of course, Mr. Arthur Hopkins is the most conspicuous example. But Mr. Hopkins, while he has given many plays such quality as no other producer could have achieved, has doubtless ruined quite as many. He has his own special flair, but for directors who are without this flair he is a dangerous example. What Mr. Hopkins has is a certain sense of the theatre in bold or spiritual directions and a nose for certain kinds of personal distinction or poignancy in actors. He has a strong magnetism that is stimulating to many artists. And he has a fine and very genuine desire that you may be free in your own soul and in your own way of expression. What he lacks is a command of the traditional theatre craft, which, though often trite and empty, constitutes nevertheless the solid basis of craftsmanship on which this, like every other art, can most securely rest. The lack of that security can at its worst prove to be disastrous.

The other extreme is the director who gives his actors their entire business, how to do every part of their rôles, even to the tone of voice; he assigns their stage positions, regulates their conceptions of the rôles, and holds the entire production tight in his own hand. No director hits this extreme, but many have the general intention of such a control and such a prescription for their results.

The advantages of this method are evident. There is a better chance for a regulated whole, for a general shape and meaning to the play when it has been translated into acting. The characters have a more just relation to one another and to the play. The rapport or exchange between the actors is more flowing and unified. There is less that is hit and miss, there are fewer gaps that arise from private temperament and chance moods. The disadvantages may include too much possibility of the mechanical, the perfunctory, the platitude, acting that has lost its spring, effects that have no relation to the person creating them.

The escape from these various disadvantages in methods will best be made through a combination of the two. There is an overseeing eye and controlling head that assigns the fortunes of each individual actor and the relationships proper to the play. But at the same time every actor may be led to express in his own terms what he has to express, and this, in so far as can be done without harm to the rest of the enterprise, may be retained, so that the actor thus uses as fully as possible that which is the medium of his art, I mean himself. Through this being alive and himself he has a better chance, perhaps, of remaining an artist rather than a puppet, and is a living part of the whole theatre art that the director works in.

Finally the director works in terms of another element in the theatre, the audience. He must consider not only what he wishes to express but also what will express it and not something else for the audience that he will speak to.

It goes without saying that if Euripides' *The Bacchae* with its theme of the redeemer God and the Dionysian release were presented for an audience of novices in a theological seminary and for an audience of rebellious young socialists, the play's meaning in each case would be different, in one case an attack on the Christian legend and in the other an encouragement to freedom or license, neither of which is Euripides' idea. *Julius Caesar* to a Moscow audience in the year of Lenin's death would spell far more of the revolutionary than it would do to a college audience in America, to whom it might mean largely an academic classicism. To secure its vitality and to express its essential quality or idea the director would have in each case to create his production within the terms of his audience. What, in a scene with nervous perturbation for its theme, might seem to an American audience rather casual than otherwise, might express something too much of jumping nerves to men of Edinburgh.

The dramatist shares the situation of all arts in that his necessity is to arouse a response by which he can create in others what he has in himself. But the dramatist writing his play knows that he can state his idea as his inspiration dictates and that it may go straight to the audience's perception or may wait ten years before its elements will be seen in the right perspective and his idea be truly perceived. The case of the director is different. His immediate audience presses in on him more closely as one of the terms in which he must work. That final theatre creation that he seeks is not so much like literature in its quality as it is like music, dancing, vivid passages in the world of nature about us; it is elusive, penetrating, it cannot wait, it cannot depend on some later memory or revisiting. He has the problem, and perhaps the thrill, of knowing that in his art, just as in human life we are alive and then gone, what he creates lives while it is before the audience, with all that living may imply—its passionate exchange, its leaping ardor and its give and take of beauty and quick impulse—and afterward has no existence at all.

❧ 11 ❧

DÉCOR

Electricity and mechanical progress have carried the theatre a long way from what it was when Aristotle was so easily able to say of the spectacle or décor that, though an attraction, it was the least artistic of all the parts of the theatrical art and had least to do with creation. The designer has become one of the important artists of the modern theatre.

There are people no doubt who would deny it, but we could say, I think, that, of all the arts, words come first as the medium by which the culture of the human race has most been handed on, or at least this is true of the Western races. Words may not be the deepest or purest, but they are the most immediate, universal and socially necessary medium of expression that we employ. Certainly it is true that, whatever may be said of them in their own spheres, painting and architecture do not come first in the theatre as mediums for conveying the idea. For a single occasion the importance of the décor will of course vary with the quality of what is to be expressed, whether it comes out best in words or music or acting or visual design. In general, the play and the acting come first; they are far ahead of the décor as means of expressing the dramatic idea.

As to the realistic settings so frequent in the theatre

of the last half century and often so costly in their demands, it is plain they are the natural children of the realistic drama and the "free theatres." The concern about realistic detail that troubles so much modern drama becomes the pride of such designers as aim to give us reality to the last item. These realistic designers wander in the same confusion as the dramatists and the public over the relation of art to nature, and much of their effort is as inconsequent, incidental and unimagined. It is obvious that the fundamental principle involved in realistic décor is the translation of the real material, such as a room or a scene, into the quality of the play. More often than not this translation does not happen; and for lack of it all those familiar stage tricks of reproduction, duplication of objects, sounds and places that excite a childish delight by being so exactly contrived, are low forms of theatre; they are not part of the dramatic moment; they stick out of themselves and thus intrude on the right dramatic content or idea.

We may object to such unrelated reproduction, or photography, as this last, since it is not art at all. To realistic décor we can have no objection when the quality it goes with is realistic—no setting could be more perfect than that the Moscow Art Theatre gave to Chekhov's *The Cherry Orchard;* it was an element in a fine theatre work in which the play, the acting, the décor and the directing all had one texture and all contributed toward a theatrical body for the informing idea. To admire realism in stage design merely because it presents some new trick or carries farther some ingenious effect of actuality is only puerile. To object to it because it is out of date or not the newest thing is superficial, faddish and idle. The necessary thing in every case, of course, is creative imagination by which the setting becomes cousin to the play.

Words cannot convey what such settings are like, but I may cite such instances as the mob scene in Reinhardt's *The Miracle*, for which Mr. Norman Bel Geddes did the design, or Mr. Robert Edmond Jones' designs for *The Hairy Ape* or *The Great God Brown*, or some design like that of Mr. Ernest de Weerth's for a drama of the French Revolution in which the form of the guillotine is present in divers lights and disguises throughout every scene, suggesting in one a doorway, in another a lattice, or a wood, a courtroom, and so on. Of this kind of décor we may say that if realism in décor can sink to mere photographic repetition and tricky claptrap, this other extreme can drop to mere obvious allegory and platitudes of stylization. In our French Revolution drama, for example, this contrivance of the guillotine form in every scene may have in it a source of power, it may unify and excite our responses. To me this design of Mr. De Weerth's was superb; but it is not in itself necessarily any more imaginative than the more photographic representation of the doorways or wood or courtroom would be. It may make more demand on the spectator's imagination if you like, since he has to conjure up for himself this diversity of places. But this extra effort on the audience's part does not imply extra imagination on the scenic artist's; if that were so the man who put a drop of water in the middle of the bare stage and made us guess that it represented the chamber in which Lady Macbeth had tried to wash the blood from her hands, would be the greatest artist in all theatre design. The trouble with symbols and stylizations is often that, when once the symbol or motif is found, it is not used with imagination, so that as soon as we have grasped the key to it, it begins to grow flat and unexpressive. Mere elimination of likeness or mere stylization need not in themselves imply anything beyond a certain novelty, if that. This confusion over what is and what is not imaginative has made a great mess in modern theatrical design.

To have an actor use a mask to show us what he is in another man's eyes as contrasted with what he is to himself when shown without the mask, may be a visual device happily suited to the play in hand, it may be in complete unity with the quality of the idea and the writing and to that extent imaginative creation. But it gets no further except in so far as the artist, at every point where the mask is used, contrives to express through it what nothing else could express so wholly. In a play where the nerves of the dramatis personae are very much awry the designer may distort the room and the furniture and even the clothes to accord with the character's state. But this invention in itself is soon exhausted, nothing in fact could be more easily hit upon than such a device and nothing could sooner lose its edge. Such a setting, if that is all it comes to, merely succeeds in getting in the dramatist's way. Nothing is more obvious than symbolism when it is poor or perfunctory. Nothing expresses less than stylization that merely tries to avoid naturalism.

There is no right way in décor, neither the stylized nor the realistic; in every case the end is the same, which is to create something that justifies itself by expressing what nothing else could quite express. When this happens in the décor, it rises to its high place in the art of the theatre. Otherwise, if it is not bad or intrusive, it may be a humble surrounding for the characters and action, a pleasant ambient that we take for granted or scarcely see.

In the modern theatre there are numberless theories major and minor of design, from a complete elimination of setting to the utmost complexity; we may have a naked stage such as Copeau used, or curtains, or the screens of Gordon Craig, or a permanent architectural background like Norman Bel Geddes' *Arabesque*, or scenes that try to copy reality to the last degree of illusion or of duplication, as in Mr. Belasco's production of *Lulu Belle*, or scenery that looks like an enlarged painting, brush strokes and all, as in Roerich's sets for *Schnegourotzka*, or constructionist design, as in the Russian *Lysistrata* or *The Man Who Was Thursday*; for all of which the files of *The Theatre Arts Monthly* afford the best record in English. In the history of theatrical décor there are many phases: the architectural setting of the Greeks: the Elizabethan stage, or at least as it has generally been represented; the elaborate baroque architecture of the seventeenth and eighteenth centuries on the Continent; the intimate interior of Molière's day; the scene painters' various but more or less undesigned efforts in the nineteenth century, and so on. All these varieties of design rest on the same basis and have the same purpose, which is to create a theatrical setting for a theatrical idea. New ideas and qualities demand a new character of design that will express their character. Types of ideas —the general conceptions characteristic of an epoch, for example—demand and evolve their fitting décor.

Each of these types of décor illustrates the same movement through many changes until the form natural to the idea is achieved, after which the movement sets in away from this form and toward a changed form for a changed content.

As has often been said, the décor depends on one man only where the rest of the production depends on many. This is most evident of course. The dramatist must rely on the actors and director, the actor on the play and the director, and the director on them; but the designer, though his idea may at the start be tampered with by the dramatist or producer, works straight when he does get to work and uses his medium directly. In one respect only must he depend on another medium: for his costumes he depends on the actor's art in wearing them, which on our stage at least is very often not far from nil. Through this one-man fact it is easy to see how we may sooner find nowadays an admirable décor at the hands of a designer than an admirable scene at the hands of the playwright, actors and director combined. I have seen few plays and little acting in late years that could be compared with some of Mr. Robert Edmond Jones' designs, and nothing else modern of any kind in the theatre that was the equal in imagination to Mr. Norman Bel Geddes' *Dante Model*. The next generation may see better plays and worse décor, or one country may now excel in one theatre element, another in another; as happened in the seventeenth century when France led in the drama of Molière and Raçine, and South Europe led in the famous baroque décor. This illustrates how uneven is the progress of the theatre art; but it is nothing against it. In any other art the several elements vary from epoch to epoch and artist to artist in excellence. For color Titian carries painting beyond Bellini but does nothing for line; and Spenser carried English poetry far ahead of his forerunners in all but narrative construction.

Settings may strike exactly the same character as the scene they contain, as in Mr. Lee Simonson's designs for *Les Ratés*, the play by Lenormand, in eleven episodes, produced by the Theatre Guild. These eleven settings were changed in less than a minute, developed from a few lines, objects and motives, just as the written scenes were, and like them expressionistic in method and direct and vivid in tone, and of the same degree of imagination and technical craft.

Or the décor provided by the designer may push the play aside; he may tend to dwarf, distort or estrange the scene by the setting he provides, as Mr. Norman Bel Geddes did with *Arabesque*. In *Arabesque* there was a scene in which the citizens of the Arabian town came in pursuit of the lover who had shamed a maiden by looking on her face unveiled. Down the steps into the court and up again and over housetops the figures streamed, covered in darkness, each with his pierced lantern whose light ran here and there over the walls and ground. Of this scene with its searching fingers of light and shadow, its flying shapes, its nuances of color, space and motion, we can say that here was a case where words could have done nothing compared to what this device achieved. In this case the ruling idea of the occasion lay in the visual part of it.

This in fact is precisely what Mr. Geddes has planned in his *Dante Model*, which he has designed for the production of a version that he would make of *The Divine Comedy*. It is certain that few instances of dramas or acting have created art of such significance as this design. And since it is a supreme instance of what visual expression may do in the theatre art, and is available for study in the edition published by the Theatre Arts Company, we may dwell on it for a moment.

The *Dante Model* calls for a circular stage, 135 feet in width and 165 feet on its longitudinal axis, and composed entirely of steps. From a central pit the slope rises on the far side to fifty feet; on the near side the slope ends in a ledge, one fourth as high, which descends toward the audience in a series of terraces until it reaches the level of the pit bottom; and there a valley runs halfway round the circle, separated from the audience by a wall seven feet high. People may pass inside this wall or on top of it. The wall ends on either side in a sort of tower which rises from the slope in a series of steps. Farther back another pair of towers or plinths rise to a height of seventy-five feet. The audience sits, as it did in a Greek theatre, in a half circle before this scene.

Mr. Geddes' arrangement of *The Divine Comedy* would not embody to any great extent that side of Dante that poets love. Nor should we have, in the drama that Mr. Geddes proposes, that terrible and penetrating immediacy that Dante has, nor that physical and spiritual precision, carried to the last and closest poetry of the soul. That might be drama too, but it is more intimate and within. What Mr. Geddes takes is that part of Dante's poem that moves toward a great essential form; what he seeks to discover is the soaring pattern of the idea. The action as he plans it would begin in long straight lines, slowly. The tempo increases, the lines are bent. The speed cannot longer be followed, the action spins round and round. There emerges the design of the soul's search and the soul's wonder and revelation. A kind of cosmic outline is discovered for the whole. Something is here revealed in motion that is like the motion of worlds, of the earth where men's lives are led, and that relates the poem to the universal. To this scope and dilation the uses of music would be brought, and light, words and variable forms, all the sides of us, all the channels by which we respond to the universe about us.

Looking at the series of photographs in the book, I could not believe that all of them, so inexhaustibly diverse, could derive from that single mass that the model is, if it were not for the earth again, whose forms, I know, have by the miracle of light the same endless variety and life. In one of the photographs— almost, I think, the most beautiful of them all—the front wall of the place is shadowed, and the forms standing on the ledge of it are black against the sea of light that lies in the pit. Beyond, and running to the base of the plinths, are the long lines of the steps; beyond them is shadow again where the upper part of the slope might be. The plinths stand in a half darkness, they are like cliffs before which the steps of a temple extend. And on the steps to one side, not far from the base of the plinth, are two figures with the light upon them. A picture this is that spreads into a grave, classical peace and at the same time a rapture, into a kind of quiet order and ecstasy, that I have not seen before. Or take the scene in fainter tones, everything in it soft and drowned in a gentle world of light. The figures stand below to the front, they extend to the top of the slope, they crowd the edges of the plinths and towers, of which the forms have softened and lost their angular details. The rear plinths seem now to be two great ships of stone come strangely into a marble harbor. And upon them cluster winged figures, as if all this were some radiant embarkation into immortal space.

And finally take that scene in which the valleys and ledges and towers have vanished and we have a sweep of silver stairs with vast shadows of wings enclosing them on either side; and in the center beyond and high up, a radiance, with two forms dimly seen in it—

> *O abbondante grazia, ond'io presunsi*
> *ficcar lo viso per la luce eterna*
> *tanto che la veduta vi concunsi!*

O abundant grace, wherein I presumed to fix my gaze on the eternal light so long that my sight was there consumed!

No one who considers the theatre and its nature, could fail to wonder what effect the décor has on the actors in a play, how much the mood that the designer creates may color, intensify, cramp, exalt, overshadow or project the actor's state of mind and his effect on the audience. We may take the work of Mr. Robert Edmond Jones as seen in the theatre or as recorded by the book published also by the Theatre Arts Company. No one could fail to wonder, looking at these designs and costumes of Mr. Robert Edmond Jones, what effect such an investiture of genius could have on the actors in the play. These actors are the immediate protagonists at hand in the drama out of life that the dramatist has given them to present. But in the vaster theatre within which the actors, the designer and the dramatist together move, the protagonists are the souls of the actors, the soul of the dramatist and the designer's soul. Within these settings that the designer provides, the business of the costumes is to reveal and ennoble the actor's part, as the actor's business is to fill them; together mutually they define and illuminate each other. And if the actor is poorer and the dramatist poorer than is good for the designer, it is his business not as it were to design down to them. Rather it is his business to express what may have been, even beyond the dramatist's own concious purpose or the actor's capacity, the nobler and living origins from which, however far off they may be, their impulse and idea have sprung.

This is the lift and fecundity, these are the conceptions at work, that we have seen in Mr. Jones' productions, in the magnificent *Birthday of the Infanta*, in *Hamlet* and elsewhere. We may take his Banquet Scene in *Macbeth*. That scene—with its fierce, ghastly colors, its light and dark, its figures of the king and queen and banqueters—not merely bold and obvious like so many designs of its type, among the Germans especially—is, for covered and insuppressible passion, quite unequaled among our stage drawings, so far as I know them; it has in it the memory of some horror when the worshipers peered into the reeking viscera of some primitive sacrifice; it is full of voices within us as old as the race, and yet it is held to the ideal mood of great drama.

To a soul, Plotinus says, in one of those passages of

his that shine on the center of our thought, is allotted its own fortunes, not at haphazard but always under a Reason, as the actors of our stage get their masks and other costumes. With the designer for the theatre it is the same. As this soul's fortunes are to it, to the designer is allotted his fortune, the drama that he is to clothe, what background of the visible world it shall be given, what garments, furniture and light. He, like this soul in Plotinus, and like this actor, adapts himself to the fortunes assigned to him, ranges himself rightly to the drama that he must invest, and to the whole principle of the piece. He too must speak out what business is given to him, exhibiting at the same time all that a soul can express of its own quality, as a singer in a song. But like this soul and like this actor, the designer holds a peculiar dignity. All three of them act in a vaster place than any stage, and have it in themselves "to be masters of all this world."

The designs of a fine artist in the décor of the theatre assume the fortunes that the dramatist has allotted to him, and express them, carrying radiantly the necessary essence of the idea. They further and reveal the meaning of the characters and the event, and convey the shock of their vitality; they sing the drama's song. But they sing the singer, too. He himself creates within the part assigned him.

◄§ 12 §►

SOUL AND BODY

WHATEVER IDEA is expressed must have a style to express it, and what does not express the idea is not its style. The idea determines the style as the hidden power of crystallization works in a mineral. Nor can the same thing be said in two different ways; each way says a different thing. This is what Buffon meant when he said that style is the man; what Spenser meant when he said that soul is form and doth the body make, and what Chaucer meant when he said the word must be cousin to the deed. In art the medium—words in literature for example—is the fund from which style borrows the substance to contain it. Out of the medium arises the body, style is the soul that animates this body.

On this basis we cannot say, as we often hear it said, that a play has a good style but no content, or that some artist or other has a good technique but nothing to say. In a way, however, we can say it; there may be such a thing as a good technique with nothing behind it. In social life certain movements and gestures, certain bows, have been developed that express certain meanings, and that can go on being used without having much content to them, they have taken on a kind of separate life of their own. In acting, likewise, there are forms, tones, gestures, phrases and characters that develop and are more or less expressive apart from much idea or sincerity behind them. When these are used we may get the vehicle itself with some aspect of vitality in it; and in fact some degree or idea or sincerity will nearly always be there. And this will be either by the artist's imitation of others, or by the excitement that the mere style itself will work on him. But even with nothing meant by it or felt within it, style might be present. It may be a sort of golden mask left by what was once alive and once expressed by it; it may be as husks, dead garments for once living fruit; or—like the corpse of the Cid on horseback that spread terror among the Moors—it may carry some of the force of its past. Style may be a sort of engine that once was vital, but that by now we had best call not technique nor style, but mechanics, certain effects that after a fashion go on working when the life has gone out of them.

Most people nowadays, talking of the theatre, have two ways of speaking of style; they either speak of it in the way painters use the word when they say that Fragonard has style, El Greco has style, as a sort of personal extra distinction or luster; or they mean by style the manner in which anything is expressed. Style in this second sense the public judges on the basis of the natural, and thinks a work of art done well in so far as it resembles life.

In the century of our grandfathers, along with that pretense of literal truth that led to a lying so odd and so antagonizing to this generation, went a mania for the natural in art. Formal gardens broke up into pretty chaos. Romantic accident in art revealed men's souls.

Painting went in for artlessness and narrative likeness.
Poetry was supposed to shun artifice, to be artless, the
child of mystery and an innocent god. These latter
years of ours, in poetry and painting both, have
brought forth schools and movements that have done
much to break down such limitations in the theory of
these arts. There are miles of modern paintings that,
however little they resemble anything in the world,
do at least stress the art's right to as much as it likes of
freedom from fact. And there are volumes of poems
that declare, and shout indeed, their technical artifice,
and make artfulness, a demonic heavenly craft of
words, their souls' release. But the art of the theatre
has gone more slowly. On the Continent there have
been schools and movements, expressionism and others,
but in America certainly less. Our main body of theatre is natural. It is based on resemblance, reproduction,
photography. Realism reigns, and confusion with regard to its theory confuses our notions with regard
to the theatre's style.

Realism, like every form and every style in art and
in nature, arises because it is expressive of something
that is to be expressed. As distinguished from the
poetic method, the realistic may be thought of as a
method in which outer details, and only outer details,
that we can actually see with our eyes and hear with
our ears, are employed to express what the artist wishes
to express; where in the poetic method anything is
allowed to the artist, whether or not it is possible or
ever seen or heard, so long as it expresses what is
desired. To say that realism shows us life as it is, became
long ago such nonsense as only a simple soul indeed
would swallow, since at the very outset there is no

is-ness to life. Realism, as much as any other method in art, selects, arranges, breathes into its material the idea that will preserve it from universal welter and chaos. There is a kind of realism to be found always that seems natural because its selection from nature and its method of treatment have long been familiar to us. There is another kind of realism, always appearing, that seems unnatural because it selects another aspect of nature, not so familiar to us in art. The hair, for example, in a statue of Michelangelo's is apt to seem more natural than in Epstein's statues, but only because we are more used to the particular style employed in the Renaissance, whose classic past has been longer with us than our own hair.

The realistic method turns on external possibility in its details; there is no other basis on which to distinguish it. For it is clear that Bernard Shaw, who uses a method of details taken from our daily and actual surface of life, is in content fantastic, fervid and poetical. Or better, take Chekhov's *The Cherry Orchard*. What soul and tremor of life arises there is no more life as it is than Shakespeare exhibits, but an impalpable inner poetry or idea, exactly as freshness wakes in us from the rain, verdure from trees, and enchantment from the night. But everyone would say that the works of Shaw and Chekhov are realistic in method, not poetic; though the line between any two methods is never fixed, and there is no right and wrong outside the work of art itself. About soliloquy in drama, for instance, we are told in textbooks that it is out of date and that in good technique it should be avoided save where it would be natural for a man to speak so to himself. It would be more pertinent and illuminative to say that save in those cases where it is quite natural, soliloquy is a sort of artifice or arrangement, a departure from the realistic, and then to say that the degree of departure of the work of art from the realistic will determine the amount of soliloquy possible. It is a question of the degree of ideality desired in the artist's representation of life; which is to say that it is a question of essential unity of style.

The point is not that one method is better than another, but that each serves to express what it alone can express—as a tree carries its own principle and a cloud its own, as music embodies its own soul and architecture its own—and so one method differs from another, just as there is one glory of the moon and another glory of the stars. The point is that realism, even great realism, is not the only way of life in the theatre.

On one hand we have realism, basing its truth on the actual surfaces of living, seeming to assume that it gives us things as they are. On the other hand is democracy, in which all are born equal, in which, as Plato says, the pupil is as good as the master, the ass as good as the rider, and everything is ready to burst with liberty. Everyone, then, being naturally familiar with things as they are and being born equal to anyone else, is a born judge of the theatre; Everyman is a full-blown critic. Nothing, so far as this Everyman can tell, is needed but for him to estimate how much this art that he observes is similar to life, not to life abundant, everlasting, and mysterious, but to the daily surface displayed to his eyes and ears. Exactly as democracy has flattered him, the politician and the wheedling press, telling the merest imbecile that he has a right to judge his government's imperialistic problem, that he even knows what he wants, so too has the realistic theory flattered him. He can tell you whether the work of the theatrical art is true or not, by comparing it with life. But the fallacy here is most obvious; we cannot assume that he can either see or hear; for the average man sees very little exactly and hears no more than he sees. To know anything quite is indeed the last thing that he will ever do, for science is farther from him than poetry.

When this man goes to the theatre, however, what is asked of him is that he bring along his eyes and ears, and nothing said about their quality. He can look from the actor to the men he has seen: truly each has two legs, he can see that. Men on the stage walk, leap, sneeze, quite as he has observed in life. No expertness of sense is asked of him; no fine hearing or sight; no culture in words with all their splendor and rarity, their power, lust, vanity, and persuasion; no tradition; no training in taste. There is no element present to put him in his place; everyone is equal. He has no ruling or dominating social idea to which he will subject the living material on the stage before him, and by which he measures it; nor on the other hand, is there in him any audacious chaos that this art must capture or arouse, terrible like the rush of the blind, ineluctable life. He is not to be obstructed with the difficult languages of style. He is not to be blocked with intellectual distinction or intimidated by cerebral rigors. He is to be made easy in the intense biological inane and very much at home in the aesthetic Zion. He has picked up a yardstick to measure things by, and it happens to be realistic. This yardstick is not his own, either; it has been given him quite as much as any other might. A theory has been put into his hands, and by it his idea of art is narrowed, his appreciation of art made dull and rambling, his response to new art forms impeded and his weak conclusions endorsed with a kind of critical approval.

We cannot say that realism is all the public will accept. When we come to the popular delights of the theatre—melodrama and vaudeville—matters are better off. In these forms of the theatre art there is stylization, violent projection, concentration, arbitrary and unphotographic method, whatever, in sum, can get the effect sought after. From these, one of our audiences gets its pleasure without remonstrance over any violation of fact or probability of likeness; it takes them as pure theatre and gets from them an inner thing, an emerging life and emotion, more or less regardless of the form that expresses it. They take it freely the way it comes. It is only when they want to be critical or theoretical that they cast about for a theory and find in the realistic the one that is readiest and easiest.

Such a theory when put to such uses limits their conceptions, distorts their approach, justifies their dullness or self-complacency, and defends their obtuseness. It succors them when they are unable to bother with a play of Sophocles'; for on the strength of it they can say that Sophocles is all artificiality and unnatural formalism. When they are blind to the power of a great visual design in stage movement or individual gesture, they can call it unnatural. It enables them to say with utter nonsense that they like Mr. Walter Hampden's *Hamlet*—which may be good or bad but

not for such a reason—because they would not know
that it was verse, so natural is it. On this realistic basis,
they are freed of operatic obligations; they can dismiss
what they are deaf and blind to in opera because
nobody would sing like that when he was fighting a
duel. It excuses them when they like best the actors
that they can feel easy with, that are just folks, that
are not so much world artists as Woodmen of the
World, democratic Rotarians.

Every epoch has its platitude. In the Elizabethan
there was the poetic platitude of borrowed finery, in-
flated images and tinsel gush of words; in the Restora-
tion, imitative chic, skimmed elegance, parade of the
naughty town; in Ibsenian realms, the moral Jeremiads
and intense, parochial personal ethics. With our theatre just now, the platitude comes out as the play of
common life. There is no harm in these little pieces
themselves. What they give us is usually a bit of popular life—a young married couple and their vicissitudes
with prosperity, parents, and simple conjugality; or
we get a kindly slice of small town life, offensive to
none, with New York and success in the offing, well
bolstered with a true girl's love. In these dramas, the
character drawing is fair up to a certain point, mostly
safe formulas of character; the incidents are friendly
and recognizable. A few popular truths are recon-
cluded, pungent comment is eluded, the social philosophy is that of newspapers, the details are taken from
the mere daily journalism of our existences. Now and
then one of these plays of common life scores an
achievement, hits something. But in general the absence
from them of all such qualities as close and revealing
style, declamation, formal arrangement, rigor and aus-

terity of idea or brilliance of mood, can but lead to disastrous ends. It means that the dramatist will be less and less able to speak except of that common or simple, or at least audible and visible, side of life that this method can express. It means that actors use only that side of their art that renders—faithfully, intensely or casually, according to the actor's talent—what we can see and hear in life and the feelings that such experience can arouse. And it means that audiences exercise in the theatre these same responses, and are engaged with recognitions, convincing verisimilitudes, duplications, and such emotions as these recognized verities can express.

We must remember that the theatre is not confined to such details and such recognizable material, but has also in it elements that have the property of music to convey pure idea, to put into us what no words can express; the ideality of architecture is an element in the theatre too; and every fertility or freedom of line, rhythm, form, and arrangement is possible to this theatrical art. The richness, the variety of the theatrical medium ends only with the complete resource of life. It is free as life is, its forms are free of all but their own expressiveness. Great realism is a fine thing in the theatre, but in so far as the realistic theory and practice lead us to forget this freedom, the realistic theory and practice must be considered, must be put in their place, be well aired, seen in their due scale, and set aside when they are unsuited to what is to be expressed.

It is no more possible to say, as many laymen and some critics did, that Duse in *Così Sia* was not good because she did not resemble an old peasant woman in either appearance or gesture, than it is possible to say

of a madonna of Rossellino's that she is not good because she does not look either Jewish or like a carpen-
ter's wife. In such a case, what is expressed is said in
terms of the human body, voice, action, gesture, presence. These are the means by which the expression is
achieved, but they are not what is expressed. Duse can
give you the peasant woman feature for feature, making the soul of her arise out of the peasant woman's
literal self, and you on your part may delight in the
precision of her resemblance and get little else, or you
may respond to the soul that she has created into these
exact details that she reproduces out of life. She can
give you the woman as remote as a figure in an early
fresco, filling in the abstract form with only ecstasy
and eternal dream; and you may receive the ecstasy
and dream of it, free of restricting recognitions, or
you may so resent the remoteness that the idea is lost.
It is at the artist's own peril and through his own necessity that he chooses his relation to the external
detail.

To miss what Duse at such a time has to say may be
for lack of the ability to understand the technical
language she speaks—the visual line, the tone, the
rhythm—is the misfortune of ignorance on your part
or of a poor natural endowment. But to have a theory
that supports you in such obtuseness is a calamity.

Take the Casket Scene from *The Merchant of Venice*, that drama of Shakespeare's that so constantly
attracts actors, and that suffers so much from the
weight of their egotisms, racisms and lack of cultural
scope. This scene is, as anyone ought to see, to vary
Shelley's line, only a pageantry of lovely ghosts on a
Venetian stream. The father's will, his daughter's oath

to marry according to the casket's choice, the love
Portia feels for Bassanio and his love for her, coming
with bright retinue to Belmont to try his fortunes for
her hand and her estates—all this, together with the
verse, the rich words, the embroidered figures and
poetic images, is of one texture. We might fall on
painting here for a help, remembering, perhaps, Simon-
ides' half true and once famed remark: "Painting is
dumb poetry and poetry speaking painting." We can
study Shakespeare's art here in the light of Veronese's.
It has no little of the quality of Veronese, a golden
masquerade of life, an arrangement, in the nuances of
which appear the sting and beauty that will delight
us and increase our living.

The easiest part of such a scene to contemplate
realistically is the story; for actions are, of course, easily seen as actual. All the productions I ever saw tried
therefore to make this story real. They always try to
give to the incidents that happen with the love, the
caskets, the suitors coming and going, a certain plau-
sibility. But to work so is to be misled by a false reality.
It is to throw the scene out by letting into one of its
elements an illusion of realistic probability. The event,
the action, is as much the artist's material as anything
else. He may use it as realistically or as remotely, as
photographically or as abstractly, as he likes. The artist has as much right to arrange and design a piece of
incident to go with his rhythmic ideas, to carry his
verse melody, to accompany his scenery, as he has to
arrange or design music or scenery to accompany his
incident. He may make a stylization, an arrangement
of his incidents quite as much as of his words, scene,
or music. The event can have the same removal and

the same quality as the writing; the events of the Trial Scene, for instance, must find their key, exactly as the Quality of Mercy speech is not the high-horse affair that most actresses, buried in red robes and stardom, make of it; it is more happily seen not as a sermon but as an aria. No one of the elements that compose the Casket Scene is more real than the other; they are all—the action as much so as any—external material through which the dramatist expresses his own idea. The scene in every respect is a work of art complete in itself, with its own essential characteristic, and free of everything outside itself; as free as Veronese's *Marriage at Cana* is of history or fact or anything but its own power and intention, by which it stands or falls.

The essence of life is that it is unceasing, ever-changing, as contrasted with what is fixed and dead, and there are as many forms in art as there are aspects of life to be expressed. The essence of style in art is that no form can be quite predicted before it comes into being, and that there is no form that is right when separated from the one content that it alone expresses, and none better or worse save with regard to the soul that is to be expressed. It does not follow that this idea will find its own style; for between it and its style lies the knack for expression. Shakespeare would doubtless never have had a style in music nor Beethoven in words. Through this knack style arrives, through the lack of it a style fails to appear. In the creations of one artist or of several, and slowly and through many changes, a style is reached that entirely expresses the idea, the style appears that is natural to it. The term *natural* means only that. And in an art the word *natural* makes sense only when it implies no binding obligation to anything outside a work of art's soul, its idea, its intentions. The work of art is not natural with regard to something else but with regard to its own nature. It approaches complete naturalness as it is free of all characteristics not its own. In this freedom the unity of its nature consists, and in this unity, as St. Augustine would have said, consists its beauty.

A work of art can be unnatural from two causes only: It may not be true to its own nature—a realistic gesture, for instance in *Oedipus King* or a formal gesture in *The Cherry Orchard*—and so does not share the quality of the idea. Or it may fail to create enough to be natural to, no nature is established. In the Copeau-Croué version of *The Brothers Karamazov*, for example, we have titanic human beings or at least human elements, insanity, love, madness and so on, in the father and the sons, and terrible events ensuing; but all these may be regarded as unnatural because of the fact that in the play as given, no life tremendous enough is created in which they could share and out of which they might arise.

We may take the acting of Madame Cécile Sorel of the Comedie Française. She knows stage manners, how to wear gowns that are remarkable creations; she has diction, voice control and a glorious and shameless exhibitionism, all valuable things in the theatre, all only with long labor acquired. People are justified in calling this art unnatural, not because it is formal, polished, sophisticated, traditional, but because it is empty. Nothing gets through that perfect enameled skin; the heart within that handsome bosom beats with the pulse of the Rue de la Paix. The burden of this divinely callous craft is only the burden of the chic. There is a hard perfection; the undismayed, decorous feet; the glisten of the scenes, nothing else; nothing is there by way of content in feeling or experience to which her technical exhibition is related.

Ideally the style in a work of art spreads throughout the whole of it; its characteristic appears in every particle. It is like a flower when you cut it through, the character, wherever you cut it, remains beautiful and alive.

❧ 13 ❧

TO THE AUDIENCE

A MAN'S STYLE is the soul that animates the body of his living. From the fund of his experience his style borrows substance to contain it. This sum of himself, his style, with all its flight, stability and wonder, is what he brings to any work of art when he responds to it and proves what meaning it shall have for him. But this work of art meanwhile has in turn its own animating soul; and unless he senses the peculiar nature of that, his response is pointless.

The theatre, like every art and like every organism that is alive, is jealous of its own nature; what belongs to it in its theatricality it takes in, absorbs, makes a part of itself; what is not its matter it expels and defeats. At our own cost we confuse the theatre with reality; for in spite of the diverse theories as to the nature of its representation of men and actions, the theatrical art remains an art, as architecture does, and is never anything else. It defeats, too, any purpose we may have of forcing it to uses not in its own nature, making it only a thesis argument, for example, or a social corrective, or a preaching vehicle, or a messenger service for personal opinion, or a museum of facts. Such matters as these it will either cast off in due time or else transmute into its own luster and pressure, as it follows its bright and singular existence.

The theatre's materials are events, characters, emotions, actions, colors, textures, words, movements, sounds. Just as the sound O gives us a different excitement from the sound I, or the circle from an oval, or marble from silk, so the materials of the theatre have expressive values in themselves. These materials are the substances that make up the theatre art. We need to respond to these various substances in the theatre, for they are the elements in it that lead us back to feeling; by which—let us not forget—we were first led to contemplate the world, and by which still—and not of itself—the world is dear and significant to us.

In the theatre, then, as in any art, we must respond to its materials in themselves. But we must also learn to discern when it is the substance that is beautiful and when the form, and when both; otherwise it would be like knowing the texture, warmth, odor, hardness and color of a body without knowing the form that the soul of it determines. In art it is the form that expresses the idea. In no art is it more difficult or more necessary than in the theatre to perceive what is the artist's material and what his idea, to distinguish between substance and form. We advance toward such a perception through an understanding of the language of the theatre art, which is the subject matter of such a book as this; we arrive at such a perception through a cultivation in ideas, in conceptions, which are the subject matter of all our living.

Around us in the world we see forms, shapes, into which characteristic forces of nature seem to have found embodiment. A tree, a horse, a flower, any one

of these fades or disappears, it goes back to dust; but
the form returns in others of its kind and is the idea
of it that remains with us. Meleager meant something
akin to that in his poem, Ὁ στέφανος περὶ κρατὶ—

> The garland fades on Heliodora's brow,
> But she shines out, garland of the garland.

We see these forms in nature, and in ourselves likewise
we desire forms, patterns of our mental world that we
call conceptions, within which our inner stream of life
finds shapes that will contain it. We would have ideas
as new bodies into which the souls of our experiences
have been reborn. We would have ideals, which are
projections, through feeling, of our intellectual pref-
erences to the completeness that we desire. It is these
ideas and complete instances brought to the service of
the theatre, that complete its function, which is to
exalt, amuse, clarify and enrich our lives, to hold up
to us the splendor and measure of time and memory
against which our lives, in their greatness, meanness,
proportion and absurdity, are led.

And finally it is by such a culture that we cure ourselves of a common fallacy in discussions of the theatre, I mean the belief that the excellence of a work of
art is measured by the number of people in the audience who understand it, an obvious absurdity, since
a feeding whistle is unanimously understood by a
whole yard of pigs. No doubt the greatest art has
at least something that can be understood by many.
But it is better to say that the test of a theatrical work
of art is not so much that everyone understands it, as
that to them who do its meaning is lofty and significant.

STARK YOUNG
Eric Bentley

The aesthetic principles are at bottom such axioms as that a note sounds good with its third and fifth, or that potatoes need salt.

All intellectual work is the same—the artist feeds the public on his own bleeding insides.

There is in the living act of perception always something that glimmers and twinkles and will not be caught, and for which reflection comes too late.

We long for sympathy, for a purely personal communication first with the soul of the world, and then with the soul of our fellows.

—William James

I: THE ARTIST AS CRITIC

A man who has written novels, poems, and plays probably will not wish to be remembered chiefly as a critic. That is to be considered a success in a secondary pursuit and a failure in the primary ones. But is criticism secondary except in the sense that it is dependent on the others: one criticizes novels, poems, and plays? Is it easier to criticize well than to write a good novel, poem, or play? Doubtless the answer to this question varies with the individual but one cannot answer with a blanket Yes. It is hard to write good criticism. Is the result less interesting for the reader? No. Nothing could be more interesting to avid readers than a page

Stark Young, 1944.

of criticism by a Samuel Johnson, a Matthew Arnold, a T.S. Eliot, an Edmund Wilson. Finally, is criticism less *important* than the literature it criticizes? Oh, dear! What I think we should do with this question is reject it. Though conceding that criticism is, if you will, a parasite upon what it criticizes, as the mistletoe upon the oak, one need not declare the result inferior. If it has less of Quality A, it has more of Quality B. The oak may be the king of the forest, yet it is the mistletoe that one kisses under at Christmas. (What would it mean, anyhow, to say: oak is better than mistletoe?)

All of this is a preamble to saying that the crown of Stark Young's creation—as of Edmund Wilson's, who also wrote poems, novels and plays—is his critical prose.

When I was young, we asked each other whether a given literary critic was a Marxist or a Freudian. Recently I was asked to contribute to a symposium in which critics would declare an allegiance to more modern schools of thought such as Structuralism and Semiotics. Following any of these trails, and others comparable, what one encounters is a claim, explicit or not, that by a given method, as like as not called methodology, literature can be rescued from mere connoisseurs and belletrists, from mere appreciators, and recorders of personal impressions: literature can now be understood and in depth.

I said I wouldn't wish to contribute to that symposium except possibly to express a dissent. I didn't see criticism being saved by any *ism* whatsoever: I would rather see criticism uncommitted to all *isms* whatsoever. Good criticism, I went on, is a matter of the critic's talent, not his philosophy, it is wholly a matter of his intelligence and his sensibility. A "correct" approach, embracing a wider, perhaps more scientific comprehension of aesthetics might seem to offer an entrée into the arts even for those lacking in intelli-

gence and sensibility. You may not respond much to
Beethoven's last quartets—your receiving apparatus
may be too crude, too closed off—but don't worry, we
can give you a vocabulary by which you can explain
those quartets as they were never explained before.
This way you fill up pages, use opaque language, make
a big intellectual impression, but you will be evading
the main issues . . .

I realized while I was giving this little lecture that
my models, among my older contemporaries, were
indeed Edmund Wilson and Stark Young, and that I
was on guard against not only certain recent developments in France but against, say, T.W. Adorno's phil-
osophic criticism in Germany, even though there are
fine personal perceptions buried in Adorno's tortured
ugly, prose. I am unfriendly to the "Yale School" of
literary scholarship of today. At least one of the Yale
professors was a better critic *before* he had a philosophy of criticism, when he was just an educated young
man who responded to poetry, using nothing more
than a traditional vocabulary and nothing other than
the traditional stock of words and notions in the field.

Criticism may often be in a parlous state but it has
never yet been rescued from that state by a philosophy
of aesthetics, nor yet by semantic adjustments, however subtle. A new phrase—Significant Form or whatever—may send a few shivers down a few spines, but
is not really an eye opener. Nothing a critic has can
open your eyes except his own eyes: he says, look! and
you look. Which sounds facile but is not. For you had
failed to look, or had not looked with sufficient concentration and discrimination. A good critic will get
you to do so.

When I ask that the traditional vocabulary be used,

I mean that criticism is intended for the non-specialist. It is good talk committed to the printed page. Presumed is a circle of talkers—the artist's audience. What they speak is English as it is spoken: English as it is not spoken is no more appropriate than, say, a language of symbols, like the pluses and minuses of the Russell-Whithead *Principia Mathematica*. Even a critic is a person. No: especially a critic is a person, and the voice of a person must be heard in all his work. Conversely, all criticism in which a human voice is not heard is bad criticism.

QUESTION: Isn't it possible that criticism might become too personal—in the sense that the person indulges himself, asks for over-particular attention, preens, poses for the cameras, over-insists that attention be paid to him?

ANSWER: Oh, what an unfair question! How could one answer it except in the affirmative. But this affirmative answer is so uninteresting.

May I advocate a style for criticism, however serious, that is not too far from the spoken word? An argument has been made for obscurity in modern literature, but when this literature is discussed by an Edmund Wilson it becomes less obscure. That is why he took pen to paper: to explain the more unknown by the less unknown. The more grandiose and doctrinaire school of modern criticism explains the unknown by the more unknown. Proust is difficult, God knows, but criticism of Proust can be even more difficult! My argument is that this is a good reason for not reading such criticism. Good criticism results from no lazy or easy-going process or mentality, but its purpose *is* to make life—the life of the student of the arts—easier. If it fails, the student is justified in taking leave of the critic and having another go at Proust. . . .

Stark Young's theater criticism rests on two principles:

1. *The autonomy of art and each work of art.*
2. *The autonomy of each of the arts, including the theater art.*

1. *The autonomy of art and each work of art.*

How can one square the statement that Stark Young stood for the autonomy of art with the notion, the knowledge, that he was famously a "Southern" critic? Edmund Wilson called him an unreconstructed Southerner, and the phrase is accurate, even in the extreme view of that time as to what "Southerner" meant: it meant of course a white Southerner who still saw himself as a Confederate soldier. If Stark Young was that kind of Southerner, would it not follow that his criticism showed a bias? Did he not favor works that such a Southerner would sympathize with? Did he not view other works in disfavor? To which one must answer yes, every critic's work reveals certain biases, and Young's was no exception. One will see him fail to bring the same sympathy to plays with one background that he brings to plays of another background. No critic is God. Still, the effort was to see each work of art in artistic terms. In intention if not always in practice, Stark Young gave every work a fair innings, a fair chance to be a work of art. Was he an aesthete? No, not if that word means art for art's sake.

Stark Young would have been quick to observe that art was for life's sake. Only it must be art. And if the critic's first duty is to report if a given work *is* art— if what was to be expressed has in fact been expressed and that in the terms of the particular art concerned. In other words, art is valid, is self-justified, doesn't have to justify itself by non-artistic criteria—whether those of a Pope or of a Commissar, whether those of Jerry Falwell or of the *New Republic's* editorial board. Each artist should be happy, should feel privileged, to serve art itself. (Yes, art is serving something. Art is serving life. And I shall come back to this later.)

What of Dante? Was he not serving the Christian religion? That, too; but not that instead. He could so easily have served the Christian religion without writing *The Divine Comedy!* If in the service of *that* religion, he created *this* poem, one asks first: has the poem been created? Is it a *poem* and not just a Christian message with aesthetic trimmings? The consensus is that, yes, it *is* a poem, and among those agreeing with this consensus are persons who do not serve that religion, persons who are not Christians. Catholicism, pragmatically speaking, is not as universal as art: for Dante has a range that goes beyond that of his Church. The human race does not accept a single theology but it seems likely that it does recognize as universal certain principles of art. In that sense, art is the true catholicism.

Art is autonomous, which is to say it is not to be judged as theology, philosophy, sociology, psychology or what not. Each work of art is autonomous, which is to say it must not be judged by pre-existent standards—"all good plays have three acts, therefore this play with two acts is bad"—but as it *turns out* to be, with the effects it *turns out* to have. Necessarily, then, it must be judged in terms of its internal relations— the relations of its parts. In taking this position already in the Nineteen Twenties, was not Stark Young the father of what in the Thirties and Forties came to be called the New Criticism, of which the worthiest as well as best-known monument is the college textbook *Understanding Poetry* by Cleanth Brooks and Robert Penn Warren?

In time the New Criticism was deluged with objections on historical grounds. Critics pointed out again and again that it was wrong to wrest works of art from their historical context and tell students they need only look at the poem on the page before them. But there's a misunderstanding here. This New Criticism did not presuppose ignorance of history. Rather it presupposed an educated reader who knew his history. What *was* being maintained was that nothing of history or any other subject could make a poem worth reading, could justify a poem's existence. To be justified, it had to exist as itself: in terms of the relation of its parts, in terms of what was there on the page, just as a piece of music had to justify itself to your ear, had to create an existence for itself by being listened to, not by being enlarged upon cerebrally and culturally, not by being related to its background, these latter processes not to be excluded but only to be postponed. You can relate a poem to its background once it has registered with you as a poem. Otherwise a bad poem, an unrealized poem, might be of more service than a good one. And indeed if one is going to rifle literature for information, why couldn't bad works of art prove more relevant and helpful than good ones?

Let's not confuse the possible documentary value of bad art with the history of good art. The history of good art can only be written by historians who appreciate the *goodness*, which is to say they have experienced it. Otherwise what you will get is the history of music by persons who have never listened to any of it. Such history is not unthinkable: it is quite easy to put together lots of information about Beethoven, or sonata form, without doing any listening, even of the most external sort. And what I'm calling "external" listening isn't of much worth either. The listening that great music deserves and requires is "internal"—i.e. it makes a demand upon the inner man, the whole man, it is a listening not only with the ear, but with the brain, and not only with the brain but with the heart.

Very well then, one must learn to look at a single work of art and observe, and respond to, all its internal relationships. This formulation perhaps suggests merely mechanical relations, or correspondence to existing customs, hardening as they do into formulae and rules. To observe which lines rhyme with which in a sonnet is certainly to observe internal relations but it is not art criticism: it is only mechanical measurement. It proves nothing artistically, as bad sonnets have the same rhyme scheme as good. Traditional French school teachers indulged a good deal in these mere mechanics: they set forth the customary modes of famous works, and exhibited the particular work only to exemplify the general rule. Thus a teacher can observe that dramas have a climax two-thirds of the way through, and can then give instances. If the pupil of such a teacher becomes a drama critic on a newspaper, he may well end up complaining that so-and-so's new play does not have its climax two-thirds of the way through. Routine criticism, bad criticism, comes about that way: approving or disapproving according to received doctrine or habitual formula.

But what the critic really needs to do is to enter into the *life* of a work of art: only then can he hope to say if the real job has been done.

What is the real job? Stark Young had an answer that is shocking in its simplicity. He said that the artist has some idea: the critic must first find out what it is and, second, estimate if it has been fully expressed in terms of the art in question—in pigment for a painter, in sound for a musician, in words only for a lyric poet, in theater for the artists who make theater. And here we must pause to note that in using an ordinary word, the word Idea, Stark Young has invited misunderstanding. Read on and you will learn that he is not talking of what is called the drama of ideas, he is not talking of the Platonic Idea (though that indeed is never far from his mind): he is using the word Idea to indicate that singleness of intention in the mind which will draw all else with it. In this sense, the painter of an entirely abstract painting may be said to have an idea: Likewise the composer of a fugue.

Here the word Singleness is just as important as the word Idea. A work of art is anything but a bundle of ideas. The last thing an artist tries to do in one work of art is toss in all the ideas he's got. Indeed, two ideas have often proved one too many, because, unless the one is subordinated to or exactly balanced against the other, they will merely compete for attention, cause confusion, prevent the work from being truly single, from having that *unum necessarium* which is Unity itself. And Stark Young will call on Plotinus and St. Augustine to endorse him here, for the doctrine of Unity is his holy of holies. If it is also a commonplace, so much the better: art can be universal because it is universally agreed that a work of art must be a Unity, and therefore that any defect in this regard will be grounds for dissatisfaction and complaint. But again one must note the futility of judging by externals. *Unity cannot be established by Unities.* Or by any external requirement. Conversely, a play by Shakespeare, brazenly disregarding the Unities, may have unity, indeed would not be a Shakespearean masterpiece if it did not.

A single idea, then, expressed in a single, unified work: this is what we are to demand. But what does it mean *expressed?* Fulfilled. In the medium concerned. The idea seeks out that medium as the appropriate one, and the medium in turn successfully offers itself as the appointed realization. Thus was stone the medium in which Rodin could realize this idea and that.

2. The autonomy of each of the arts, the autonomy of the theater art.

Each art, Stark Young liked to say, should be doing what it *alone* can do. So the true philosopher would contemplate what stone has expressed for Rodin, paint for Cézanne, music for Bach, and so on. What of the theater art? People of my background have tended to see it as literature wired for sound and latterly wired also for the TV screen. In other words, performance tended to be viewed, by literary people at least, as just a transmission apparatus like a telephone.

Bernard Shaw, for instance, viewed movies as merely a way to reach a wider audience, not as the adaptation of his work to the ways and means of another art.

When I first heard of Stark Young, he was on the staff of a magazine called *Theatre Arts* and what most of us imbibed from that monthly magazine was the view that theater wasn't just one art, literature, it was several: it was music, it was stage design, it was acting and directing. One art was added to another. The various arts were piled on one another. A rich potpourri! This, however, is not the doctrine of Stark Young.

Equality was not a favorite notion for him, and certainly he did not preach that, in theater, the various arts were equal. What he did say is continuous with the theory I have been expounding. If each art is unique, then theater is not literature. But if theatre is unique, then it has a character of its own: is one thing, not several things. Those several arts have to be combined in a unity, and, if this is not a union of equals, then some sort of ranking order will be discerned—*dis*-order being inconsistent with the over-all principle of unity. In this ranking order Stark Young puts the playwright first. Second comes the actor, and in one respect he is first: he comes at the spectator first, is that which the audience confronts *in the first instance.* To the extent that some plays are actor-proof, the director too might move into first position. To the extent that a play is weak, but susceptible of rare spectacle, the set designer and costumer might, exceptionally, move into first position. . . .

Now here comes an essential part of the theory which perhaps even today has not been fully absorbed, though it follows quite smoothly from Stark Young's premises. Although the playwright is the master mind of dramatic theater, the actor is not a telephone transmitting his dialogue, nor yet even a semaphorist signalling his gestures. He is a person. He is an artist, and as such a maker of art, a creator of something new. True, this something new can be, should be, an interpretation of what the playwright has written. But an interpretation that is also a work of art is itself unique, therefore different from, distinct from, what it interprets. Again the principle of the single idea applies. The actor of Hamlet does not merely add one line to another, "interpreting" each line as he goes along, thus arriving at The Interpretation by aggregation. That would only be improvisation. The actor has studied the role. He has absorbed it as he *can*, that is to say, as he *is*. It is rash, as Stark Young often pointed out, to say: this actor *became* Hamlet. No, he remained himself. Only a god like Proteus becomes someone else. A human being establishes points of contact: finds what, in his own personality, can be used to express what Shakespeare has written. What Proteus would come up with one might call the Platonic idea of the role. But of the human actor one cannot even say that he should get as near this as he can, for that is not how your human actor works. He is not a dybbuk climbing inside someone. He is an artist making . . . *something new.* Something new that he hopes the author might endorse if he were around but which in any case must be a dovetailing of Shakespeare's unique piece of writing with his own unique personality and unique artistry. "Dovetailing" is an ill phrase if what it suggests is pastiche. The final result must be single. The actor cannot invade and annex Hamlet, but he has an idea of Hamlet and he can express it. Ideally speaking. And this, not mere subordination to Shakespeare, *is* the ideal. If less is achieved, it will be for the critic to point out that the idea is but imperfectly expressed or, worse still, that the actor's idea is itself unworthy, misleading, even dead wrong.

So what is required of the theatre critic? The perspicacity to read the idea in the performance, and the tact to sense if it is fully expressed and in what details, by what means, by what surprising line-readings, by what unpredicted movements. What the critic must not do is accept or reject these movements, these line-readings, on their own—as being traditional or the reverse, as being handsome or brilliant or the reverse. He must see them, feel them, as part of a pattern, the pattern that expresses (if all is well) the pervasive idea.

I am re-stating what I have taken to be the two main principles of Stark Young's theatre criticism. In essence they are traditional, even perennial, nor are they unduly complex. Nonetheless they remain beyond the grasp of most dramatic critics, who seem incapable of the discipline required, the intellectual labor required, and instead blurt out their immediate reactions to the separate parts of the theatre occasion. They register only a brute response to each moment, or perhaps only to certain moments, the moments when they are awake. And since such waking moments follow minutes of somnolence, one senses the lack of connection with what has been going on. Our critics are accustomed to let themselves be as passive as the most helpless, hapless spectator. "Show me!" "Entertain me!" Alas, extreme passivity simply inhibits all real artistic experience. When Walt Whitman said that for great art you need great audiences, he meant, I should think, that the spectators ought to be artists, too, people willingly a part of the artistic experience, bringing to the event eagerness, curiosity, intelligence. . . . The ideal spectators I find myself dreaming of here would of course all be critics. Criticism doesn't have to be written down. What, following in Stark Young's footsteps, I've been defining as the critic's attitude is only the ideal spectator's attitude. I'm dreaming of a wakeful, alert audience that would grasp an idea and figure if it was being properly expressed.

II: THE ARTIST AS MAN

I had not followed Stark Young's career at *The New Republic* before World War II—I was too young for that—but I picked up the books on theatre that he had brought out in the Twenties and mentioned them in my first book on theatre, *The Playwright as Thinker*, 1946. Stark Young was to retire from *The New Republic* in '47 but he wrote a long review of my book a few months before that happened. Re-reading it today I find him in two minds about the younger critic: I couldn't have been that good if I was also that bad! On the one hand, he says the book is "worth reading," nay, "excellent," and "manages to say a surprising lot, and amid so much knowledge, scope and even prophecy, to omit vast quantities of nonsense and vapor." On the other hand, he pushes it away as minor and external to its real subject, which is art. In an attempt to sum up, he says that the book has range, and that he can't do justice to it, the book is so ambitious, but he does think he has found its weak spot:

. . . the bright shortcoming in the book is the author's lack of knowledge of the theater . . . I gather from the text that his presence at some theatre occasion would be worth little, though he might be good, taking the play as itself solely, on the future or the past for it. You can tell, from what he says about various plays, that he has never seen them produced . . . There are many moments in great drama where the actor's voice would be the final test of the moment's power, but Mr. Bentley does not know that.

Stung by these comments, I was determined to prove that I did know—or would get to know—the theater. Hitherto—Stark Young had guessed right—I had done hardly any theater criticism: Yale kept me too busy studying for a Ph.D. in comparative literature. But I was now able to get myself invited to write a mini-manifesto about theater and its critics on the occasion of a visit to New York by the Old Vic of London. It contains a long paragraph about Stark Young in which *I* am of two minds about *him.* In his review of me, he had stressed my youth, and in this retort of mine I find him old and tired and nostalgic. He is living with the theater's past whereas one must think of its future and, if one writes on it, live with its present, etc., etc. On the other side, I find him worth reading and the best dramatic critic around.

It was this piece, entitled "The Old Vic, the Old Critics, and the New Generation,"* that brought me the first of those letters from Stark Young that would much later find their place in John Pilkington's two-volume *Stark Young, a Life in the Arts.* It was a long letter with many interesting and characteristic things in it, yet what has stuck most clearly in my memory is that Stark Young had cut out paragraphs of my

*Published, by the way, in *View,* the only New York magazine of that era which one might plausibly have labeled "gay."

piece and scribbled on them. One scrawl read "two times two is four"—this was written on top of my excoriation of the Broadway critics. He didn't disagree with my diatribe but to him such things were not worth bothering about. In his review of *The Playwright*, he had agreed with my refutation of some argument or other by Allardyce Nicoll but had made it clear he didn't think Allardyce Nicoll worth refuting. Here you may sense the distance between the veteran artist who had fled Academia three decades earlier, and the young Assistant Professor who considered himself rather bold in taking on the leading academic in his field. At the time Nicoll was Dean of the Yale School of Drama.

The important thing for me was that Stark Young's letter brought us face to face for the first time. After which, acquaintance grew to friendship. Professionally, we now became a mutual admiration society. I dedicated a book to him, and he did something more unusual: in a re-issue of a book of his, he deleted the name of the original dedicatee and replaced it with mine.

Of the private Stark Young I don't wish to say much more than that he is still in the shadows. He withheld a large and central part of himself both from his novels and from his letters. It was my privilege to make contact with that private life and at least glimpse some of its joys and its agonies, its triumphs and its failures, its realizations and its errors.

But there is a point I wish to make about Stark Young's work which is intimately related with the self which he kept hidden. I disagree with those who find Stark Young precious, over-elegant, dandified. They would have a real point only if the elegance of his writing were a self-contained thing, if his work were all surface and gave no sense of what was under that surface. Even without knowing his life, I think you can gather something else from the writing, and especially from the best of it. The qualities he achieved in his prose are a triumph over equal and opposite qualities in life, and indeed, if one is to understand Stark Young, I think one will do so *in terms of opposites*. What he thought of the world you could figure by reversing what he says about high art or what he himself makes by way of high art. Why the enormous emphasis on beauty and soul? Because this world is ugly and soulless. Why the passionate love of intellectual clarity, of simplicity? Why the predilection for high style, why the consistent attempt to achieve it? Because the world is a mess, a chaos, complex and untidy beyond all comprehension, because our life and work are styleless, undistinguished, paltry.

It has been said of Ernest Hemingway that his prose at its best seems written in the state of tension of someone who knows he has only hours to live, and indeed we now understand that Hemingway lived for years with such a sword hanging over him, a sword his father had already used, and which, alas, Ernest would use long before he had lived out his time. In Stark Young's work, I don't feel it is death that waits in the wings, I think it is pain, psychic pain, unbearable anxiety threatening to overpower and overwhelm with its manic message: CHAOS IS COMING AGAIN.

And so qualities that keep us from being hurt are the qualities that above all else are sought after. *"Qualities that keep us from being hurt."* I have taken the phrase from Stark Young. From the heart of Stark Young. What is there is a sense of hurt. I must report that this is what I felt in the man I met and then learned to know and then learned to love. The beauty he sought to create, like the beauty he doted on in Italy and Greece, in the Old South or in the furnishing of his New York apartment, was what he turned to for help: his life belt. The key to his character, if there is a single key to so large, subtle and mysterious an entity, is what he turned *from*, what he averted his gaze from, what he fled from in something akin to panic.

Back in the years that have been called the Red Decade, Stark Young would sometimes be spoken of as an escapist. The implication that he escaped all reality is false, yet the movement of his will and imagination—and these do move in one direction or another, at one speed or another—is quite accurately described as flight, as at least attempted escape. For Stark Young, the heart of darkness was not out there on an alien continent at the end of a long journey, it was here in Mississippi, it was there in New York, it was universally *of our time*, it was *now*. Which begins to explain why Stark couldn't help making any previous age something of a Blessed Isle: after all, he had fled to it in search, if not of final bliss, at least of relief —release from intolerable pain.

If there is any point in John Pilkington's expositions of Stark Young's views where I venture a partial dissent, it is where he connects Young with "Christian humanism." I did not find him religious: he fled so fast, the hound of Heaven couldn't catch up with him. Instead of religion he had two things. The first was Art—all the arts—which he embraced with the fervor

which the religious give to God. "A life in the arts,"
yes: Stark Young dwelt with beauty as a saint dwells
with goodness. . . . The second thing was Love, and
not of God, but of people. In no one I have ever met
was the life of the affections more spontaneous and
abundant. How he loved to love! In an age when we
consider the critic cold, and the intellectual with-
drawn, he was the warmest and most outgoing of men.
Is that Southern courtesy? I would say it is much more
than courtesy, it is *hospitality* in its elemental form:
making people feel at home because your arms are
open to them and you want them: you love them.
Stark Young had a genius for loving which made it
easy for him to include ever new people in the circle
of the beloved. But three persons were privileged beyond the others: his sister Julia, his nephew Stark, and
his lover "Wales" Bowman. The published letters bear
eloquent and lovely witness to the first two of these
loves. In view of the mores of those times, the third
had to be hidden, but let those who would understand
Stark Young make due allowance for it. If I have
placed a primary stress on what he fled from, I would
also call attention to what he fled to: to beauty and to
a love that was not supernatural but for him . . . natural.

Escapism was a dirty word because it implied the
escaping of all the realities. Stark Young did exclude
a lot. I think he felt he had to, to keep sane. His friends
sometimes wished to reform him, correct his opinions,
fill in the gaps in his knowledge. For it wasn't just
modern philistinism he rejected. He rejected most of
modern art and literature. His impulse was to reject
the whole modern age, and upon mature considera-

tion one sees this as itself a modern phenomenon. Stark Young was not a character in *So Red the Rose.* On the contrary! He fled *in fantasy* to that world, and the vehemence of the flight gives it its glamour, its intensity, without in my view concealing that the novel is, for all the many pure facts inserted therein, a fantasy. If I were to suggest a theory of Stark Young's life and work, it would be that while his direct treatments of reality—his novels and plays—often tended too much toward fantasy, where he was absolutely real, where he was firmly in command of reality, was in his treatment of those "fantasies" which we call the arts, and particularly that Super-fantasy the theater art.

Let me add one more thing to my account of his philosophy of theatre. Had he really been an escapist, an aesthete in the usual sense, he would have made the theater into an ivory tower, into that castle of Axel in which it was said, "As for living, our servants will do that for us." But Stark Young was no more of an aesthete than he was an ascetic. He believed in living up to the hilt. And he did live up to the hilt: one feared for him, so eagerly and totally did he give of himself. Therein lay both his strength and his vulnerability. He did not live apart: he lived on East 57th Street in New York City. He did not wish a life apart for the arts, either. Art was not, I repeat, for art's sake, it was for life's sake. It had a purpose: to improve the quality of living.

In that masterpiece, *The Theatre,* where the topic is the director, Stark Young wrote:

The glory of the theater is that it comes so close to human life that it breaks up into all our channels of response and expression: all are alive together and through all the whole sum appears. This insight into the revealing power of each of these theater mediums amounts after all only to the director's being alive in it. Through these diverse avenues he seeks life for what he desires to create, exactly as in our daily experience we look at one thing and listen to another, or as we fling ourselves on words, on song or color, on rhythm, action, ideas—sowing ourselves on every wind—in order to create ourselves in terms of living.

Certainly this man *created himself* not in terms of art only but in terms of living. He flung himself on words, on song, on color, on rhythm, action, ideas. He sowed himself on every wind.